INTRODUCTORY LEVEL

MA1

Management Information

EXAM KIT

MA1: MANAGEMENT INFORMATION

A catalogue record for this book is available from the British Library.

Published by Kaplan Publishing UK
Unit 2 The Business Centre
Molly Millars Lane
Wokingham
Berkshire
RG41 2QZ

ISBN 978-1-78740-335-2

© Kaplan Financial Limited, 2018

Printed and bound in Great Britain

Acknowledgements

We are grateful to the Association of Chartered Certified Accountants, the Chartered Institute of Management Accountants and the Institute of Chartered Accountants in England and Wales for permission to reproduce past examination questions. The answers have been prepared by Kaplan Publishing.

The text in this material and any others made available by any Kaplan Group company does not amount to advice on a particular matter and should not be taken as such. No reliance should be placed on the content as the basis for any investment or other decision or in connection with any advice given to third parties. Please consult your appropriate professional adviser as necessary. Kaplan Publishing Limited and all other Kaplan group companies expressly disclaim all liability to any person in respect of any losses or other claims, whether direct, indirect, incidental, consequential or otherwise arising in relation to the use of such materials.

All rights reserved. No part of this publication may be reproduced, stored in a retrieval system, or transmitted, in any form or by any means, electronic, mechanical, photocopying, recording or otherwise, without the prior written permission of Kaplan Publishing.

These materials are reviewed by the ACCA examining team. The objective of the review is to ensure that the material properly covers the syllabus and study guide outcomes, used by the examining team in setting the exams, in the appropriate breadth and depth. The review does not ensure that every eventuality, combination or application of examinable topics is addressed by the ACCA Approved Content. Nor does the review comprise a detailed technical check of the content as the Approved Content Provider has its own quality assurance processes in place in this respect.

Kaplan Publishing are constantly finding new ways to make a difference to your studies and our exciting online resources really do offer something different to students looking for exam success.

This book comes with free MyKaplan online resources so that you can study anytime, anywhere. This free online resource is not sold separately and is included in the price of the book.

Having purchased this book, you have access to the following online study materials:

CONTENT	ACCA (including FFA, FAB, FMA)		FIA (excluding FFA, FAB, FMA)	
	Text	Kit	Text	Kit
Eletronic version of the book	✓	✓	✓	✓
Check Your Understanding Test with instant answers	✓			
Material updates	✓	✓	✓	✓
Latest official ACCA exam questions*		✓		
Extra question assistance using the signpost icon**		✓		
Question debriefs using clock icon***		✓		
Consolidation Test including questions and answers	✓			

* Excludes AB, MA, FA, LW, FAB, FMA and FFA; for all other subjects includes a selection of questions, as released by ACCA
** For ACCA SBR, AFM, APM, AAA only
*** Excludes AB, MA, FA, LW, FAB, FMA and FFA

How to access your online resources

Kaplan Financial students will already have a MyKaplan account and these extra resources will be available to you online. You do not need to register again, as this process was completed when you enrolled. If you are having problems accessing online materials, please ask your course administrator.

If you are not studying with Kaplan and did not purchase your book via a Kaplan website, to unlock your extra online resources please go to www.mykaplan.co.uk/addabook (even if you have set up an account and registered books previously). You will then need to enter the ISBN number (on the title page and back cover) and the unique pass key number contained in the scratch panel below to gain access.

You will also be required to enter additional information during this process to set up or confirm your account details.

If you purchased through Kaplan Flexible Learning or via the Kaplan Publishing website you will automatically receive an e-mail invitation to MyKaplan. Please register your details using this email to gain access to your content. If you do not receive the e-mail or book content, please contact Kaplan Publishing.

Your Code and Information

This code can only be used once for the registration of one book online. This registration and your online content will expire when the final sittings for the examinations covered by this book have taken place. Please allow one hour from the time you submit your book details for us to process your request.

Please scratch the film to access your MyKaplan code.

Please be aware that this code is case-sensitive and you will need to include the dashes within the passcode, but not when entering the ISBN. For further technical support, please visit www.MyKaplan.co.uk

INTRODUCTION

Packed with exam-type questions, this book will help you to successfully prepare for your exam.

- In this exam kit you will find questions that are of exam standard and format – this will check and further develop your subject knowledge, as well as enable you to master the examination techniques.

- A mock exam is at the back of the book – try it under timed conditions and this will give you an idea of the way you will be tested in your actual exam.

- All questions are grouped by syllabus topics

Real exams for FIA MA1 are not published as questions are reused.

CONTENTS

	Page
Index to questions and answers	P.7
Syllabus and revision guidance	P.9
The Examination	P.11

Section

1	Multiple-choice questions	1
2	Answers to multiple choice questions	51
3	Mock exam questions	83
4	Answers to mock exam questions	97
5	Specimen exam	

Quality and accuracy are of the utmost importance to us so if you spot an error in any of our products, please send an email to mykaplanreporting@kaplan.com with full details.

Our Quality Co-ordinator will work with our technical team to verify the error and take action to ensure it is corrected in future editions.

INDEX TO QUESTIONS AND ANSWERS

MULTIPLE-CHOICE QUESTIONS

Page number

	Questions	Answers
The nature and purpose of cost and management accounting	1	51
Source documents and coding	6	55
Cost classification and measurement	9	57
Cost accounting	19	62
The spreadsheet system	37	75

SYLLABUS AND REVISION GUIDANCE

Syllabus content

No prior knowledge is required before commencing study for Paper MA1.

Candidates require a sound understanding of the methods and techniques covered in this paper to enable them to move on to the more complex systems and management control problems covered at subsequent levels.

Some of the methods introduced in this paper are revisited and extended in Paper MA2.

DETAILED SYLLABUS

A   THE NATURE AND PURPOSE OF COST AND MANAGEMENT ACCOUNTING
Chapters 1 and 2
1. Nature of business organisation and accounting systems
2. Management information

B   SOURCE DOCUMENTS AND CODING
Chapters 4-7
1. Sources of information
2. Coding system

C   COST CLASSIFICATION AND MEASUREMENT
Chapter 3, 8 and 10
1. Cost classification
2. Cost units, cost centres, profit centres and investment centres

D   RECORDING COSTS
Chapters 5, 6, 7 and 9
1. Accounting for materials
2. Accounting for labour
3. Accounting for other expenses
4. Accounting for product costs

E   THE SPREADSHEET SYSTEM
Chapter 11
1. Spreadsheets overview
2. Creating and using spreadsheets
3. Presenting and printing spreadsheet data/information

Key areas of the syllabus

All areas of the syllabus are equally important.

MA1 : MANAGEMENT INFORMATION

Planning your revision

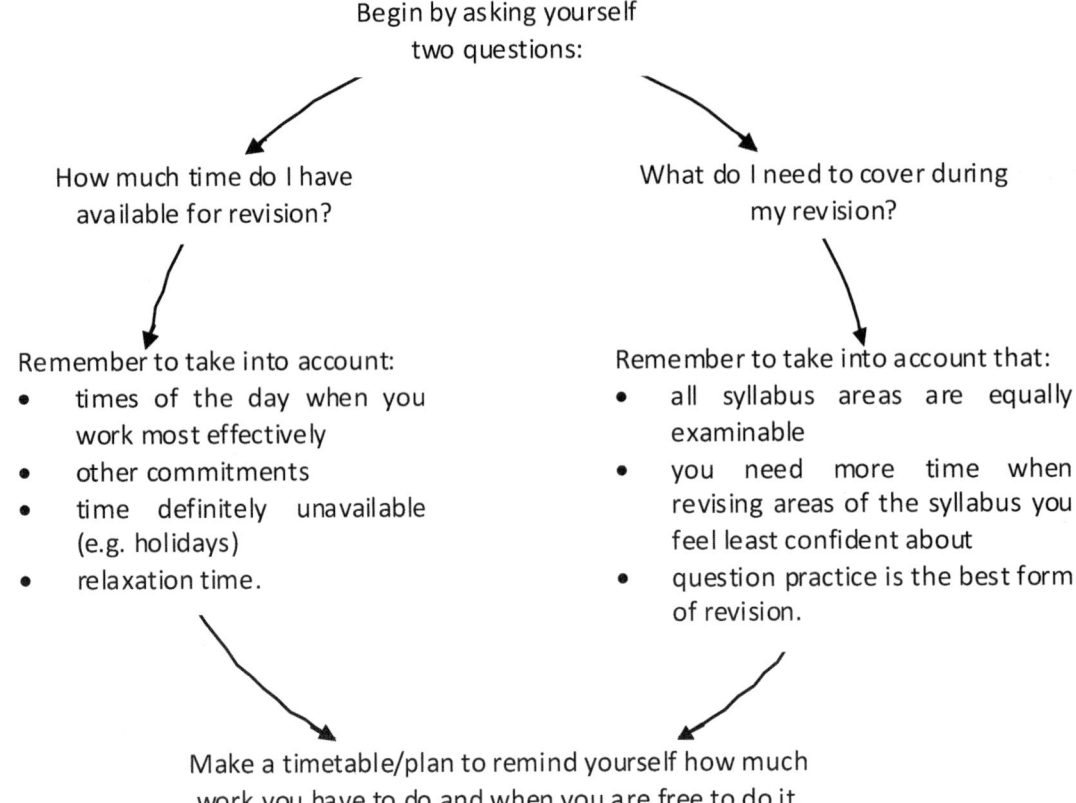

Revision techniques

- Go through your notes and textbook **highlighting the important points.**
- You might want to produce your own set of **summarised notes.**
- **List key words** for each topic to remind you of the essential concepts.
- **Practise exam-standard questions**, under timed conditions.
- **Rework questions** that you got completely wrong the first time, but only when you think you know the subject better.
- If you get stuck on topics, **find someone to explain** them to you (your tutor or a colleague, for example).
- **Read recent articles** on the ACCA website or in the student magazine.
- **Read** good newspapers and professional journals.

THE EXAMINATION

Format of the exam

You can sit this exam as a paper-based or computer-based exam.

	Number of marks
50 multiple-choice questions (2 marks each)	100
Time allowed: 2 hours	

Answering the questions

- **Multiple choice questions** – read the questions carefully and work through any calculations required.
- **If you don't know the answer**, eliminate those options you know are incorrect and see if the answer becomes more obvious. Remember that only one answer to a multiple choice question can be right!
- **If you get stuck with a question** skip it and return to it later.
- **Answer every question** – if you do not know the answer, you do not lose anything by guessing. Towards the end of the examination spend the last five minutes reading through your answers and making any corrections.
- **Equally divide the time** you spend on questions. In a two-hour examination that has 50 questions you have about 2.4 minutes per a question.
- **Do not skip any part of the syllabus** and make sure that you have *learnt* definitions, *know* key words and their meanings and importance, and *understand* the names and meanings of rules, concepts and theories.
- Bear in mind that this paper is biased towards narrative rather than computational questions, essentially testing knowledge rather than application.

Computer-based examinations

- Be sure you understand how to use the **software** before you start the exam. If in doubt, ask the assessment centre staff to explain it to you.
- Questions are **displayed on the screen** and answers are entered using keyboard and mouse. At the end of the exam, you are given a certificate showing the result you have achieved.
- **Don't panic** if you realise you've answered a question incorrectly – you can always go back and change your answer.

Section 1

MULTIPLE CHOICE QUESTIONS

THE NATURE AND PURPOSE OF COST AND MANAGEMENT ACCOUNTING

1 Which of the following features are characteristic of an integrated accounting system?

    1   Management accounting and financial accounting ledger accounts are held in the same ledger.

    2   There are no individual ledger accounts for receivables or payables.

    3   Transactions are coded for both financial accounting purposes and management accounting purposes.

    A   1 only

    B   1 and 2 only

    C   1 and 3 only

    D   2 and 3 only

2 Which of the following qualities is *not necessarily* a quality of good information?

    A   It should be relevant

    B   It should be understandable

    C   It should be worth more than it costs to produce

    D   It should be available quickly

3 Which of the following definitions best describes 'information'?

    A   Data that consists of facts and statistics before they have been processed.

    B   Data that consists of numbers, letters, symbols, events and transactions which have been recorded but not yet processed into a form that is suitable for making decisions.

    C   Facts that have been summarised but not yet processed into a form that is suitable for making decisions.

    D   Data that has been processed in such a way that it has a meaning to the person who receives it, who may then use it to improve the quality of decision making.

MA1 : MANAGEMENT INFORMATION

4   Which of the following is *not* a purpose of management information in a company?

- A   To provide records of current and actual performance
- B   To compare actual performance with planned performance
- C   To help management with decision making
- D   To inform customers about the company's products

5   Which of the following is *not* correct?

- A   Cost accounting can be used for inventory valuation to meet the requirements of internal reporting only
- B   Management accounting provides appropriate information for decision making, planning, control and performance evaluation
- C   Routine information can be used for both short-term and long-run decisions
- D   Financial accounting information can be used for internal reporting purposes

6   Which of the following are *all* qualities of good management information?

- A   Digital, brief, relevant
- B   Reliable, consistent, timely
- C   Secure, accurate, printed
- D   Accessible, universal, complete

7   Which of the following statements is *incorrect*?

- A   Management accounting reports are more accurate than financial accounting statements.
- B   Management accounting reports are more detailed than financial accounting statements.
- C   Management accounting reports are more frequent than financial accounting statements.
- D   Management accounting reports are not disclosed to shareholders and investors.

8   Which one of the following is always a quality of good information?

- A   Immediate availability
- B   Availability to everyone
- C   Reliable
- D   Technically accurate

9   Which one of the following statements is correct?

- A   Data is held on computer in digital form whereas information is in a form that is readable to human beings.
- B   Information is obtained by processing data.
- C   Data and information mean the same thing.
- D   Data consists of numerical or statistical items of information.

MULTIPLE CHOICE QUESTIONS : SECTION 1

10 Which of the following items of information might be produced by a management accounting system?

- A Income tax deducted from employees' wages and salaries
- B Amounts of money owed to suppliers
- C Current bank balance
- D Profitability of product items

11 Which of the following is an example of external information that could be used in a management accounting system?

- A Consumer price index statistics
- B Price list for the products sold by the business
- C Production volume achieved by the production department
- D Discounts given to customers

12 Which of the following is *not* management accounting information?

- A Sales budget
- B Variance report
- C Payroll report
- D Profitability report

13 Which of the following items would be included in the financial accounting system but not in the management accounting system?

- A Sales commissions payable to sales representatives
- B Costs of repairs to the office air conditioning system
- C Profits paid out in dividends to the business owners
- D Direct labour costs

14 Why is management information valuable for decision making?

- A It enables management to make the correct decision
- B It helps management to reach a more informed decision
- C It can be used to allocate blame if a poor decision is made
- D It enables managers to make decisions more quickly

15 Which of the following statements about office manuals is *not* correct?

- A They are particularly useful for dealing with out-of-the-ordinary situations
- B They can be used to check on the correct procedures in cases of doubt
- C They can be used to help with the training of new staff
- D They help to maintain standards of performance

MA1 : MANAGEMENT INFORMATION

16   What is a prime entry record in an accounting system?

   A   A record of an important transaction, usually a high-value transaction

   B   An entry in the ledger accounts

   C   The first record of a transaction entered into the accounting system

   D   A record of direct materials, direct labour and direct expenses costs

17   Which of the following statements are correct?

   1   In a system of interlocking accounts, financial accounts and management accounts are recorded in the same ledger.

   2   The number of errors in a computerised accounting system should be less than if a manual accounting system is used.

   3   Transactions should be recorded more quickly in a computerised accounting system than in a manual accounting system.

   A   Statements 1 and 2 only are correct

   B   Statements 1 and 3 only are correct

   C   Statement 2 only is correct

   D   Statements 2 and 3 only are correct

18   Which of the following best describes double entry bookkeeping?

   A   A manual system of recording accounting transactions

   B   A system of recording business transactions in ledgers

   C   A system of recording an accounting transaction twice in the main ledger

   D   A system of management accounting

19   Which of the following would be classified as data?

   A   Number of purchase requisitions

   B   Analysis of wages into direct and indirect costs

   C   Table showing variances from budget

   D   Graph showing the number of labour hours worked

20   Which of the following are primary data?

   (i)   Information on timesheets used for making up wages.

   (ii)   Information from a government publication concerning forecast inflation rates used for budgeting.

   (iii) Information from a trade publication used to choose a supplier of raw materials.

   A   (i) and (ii)

   B   (i) and (iii)

   C   (i) only

   D   (i), (ii) and (iii)

21 Which of the following is a feature of financial accounting information?

   A   It is used to calculate the cost of a product or service
   B   Limited companies are required by law to prepare this information
   C   It is concerned with future results as well as historical information
   D   The benefit must exceed the cost and it must be relevant for purpose

22 What is the scientific term for facts, figures and information?

   A   Consultancy
   B   Data
   C   Referencing
   D   Statistics

23 Which one of the following is true with regard to management information?

   A   It is the same as operating information
   B   It must be produced by a computer
   C   It should be completely accurate, regardless of cost
   D   It should be produced if its cost is less than the increased revenue to which it leads

24 Which one of the following is an example of internal information for the wages department of a large company?

   A   A Code of Practice issued by the Institute of Directors
   B   A new national minimum wage
   C   Changes to tax coding arrangements issued by the tax authorities
   D   The company's employees' schedule of hours worked

25 Which one of the following would be included in the financial accounts, but may be excluded from the cost accounts?

   A   Bank interest and charges
   B   Depreciation of storeroom handling equipment
   C   Direct material costs
   D   Factory manager's salary

26 What is the most appropriate definition of an office?

   A   A centre for exchanging information between businesses
   B   A centre for information and administration
   C   A place where information is stored
   D   A room where many people using IT work

27 Which one of the following is a disadvantage of office manuals?

- A Strict interpretation of instructions creates inflexibility
- B The quality of service received from suppliers is reduced
- C They create bureaucracy and demotivate staff
- D They do not facilitate the induction and training of new staff

28 Which one of the following is least likely to be carried out by an Accounts Department?

- A Arrangement of payment of payables
- B Calculation of wages and salaries to be paid
- C Despatch of customer orders
- D Preparation of company financial records

29 What is the main purpose of prime entry records?

- A to calculate the cash received and spent by a business
- B to prevent a large volume of unnecessary detail in the ledgers
- C to provide a monthly check on the double entry bookkeeping
- D to separate the transactions subject to sales tax from those that are exempt

SOURCE DOCUMENTS AND CODING

30 Which of the following is usually responsible for preparing a delivery note?

- A Buyer
- B Supplier
- C Stores manager
- D Accountant

31 Which of the following is in the correct chronological sequence for sales documents?

- A Enquiry – Order – Invoice – Payment
- B Order – Enquiry – Invoice – Payment
- C Enquiry – Order – Payment – Invoice
- D Enquiry – Invoice – Order – Payment

32 Which of the following is in the correct chronological sequence for purchase documents?

- A Purchase order – Invoice – Goods received note – Delivery note
- B Delivery note – Goods received note – Purchase order – Invoice
- C Purchase order – Delivery note – Goods received note – Invoice
- D Goods received note – Delivery note – Purchase order – Invoice

MULTIPLE CHOICE QUESTIONS : SECTION 1

33 Which of the following documents should be checked before a purchase invoice is paid, to confirm that the price and quantities are correct?

	Price check	Quantity check
A	Purchase order	Purchase order
B	Goods received note	Delivery note
C	Purchase invoice	Goods received note
D	Purchase order	Goods received note

34 You are the accountant responsible for the input into the computer accounting system of data about goods received from suppliers. For each transaction, you require a copy of the purchase order, delivery note, goods received note and invoice.

Where are you most likely to find the code number for an item of inventory for entering in the system?

- A   Purchase order
- B   Delivery note
- C   Goods received note
- D   Invoice

35 Which one of the following is *least* likely to be carried out by the accounts department?

- A   Collecting money receivable from credit customers
- B   Receiving goods from suppliers into store
- C   Processing expenses claims
- D   Arranging payments of tax to the tax authorities

36 Hockey Skill operates from three main sites. In analysing its costs (overheads) it uses a nine digit coding system. A sample from the coding manual shows:

Site		Expenditure type		Function	
Whitby	100	Rent	410	Purchasing	600
Scarborough	200	Power	420	Finance	610
York	300	Heat and light	430	Production	620
		Travel costs	500	Sales	630
		Telephone and postage	520		

The order of coding is: site/expense/function

How would an invoice for the Whitby site for power be coded?

- A   100/420/600
- B   100/420/620
- C   100/420/610
- D   100/430/610

KAPLAN PUBLISHING

MA1 : MANAGEMENT INFORMATION

37 In accounting systems, data is usually organised using codes.

Which one of the following statements about codes is *incorrect*?

- A Using codes helps to improve the speed and accuracy of data processing.
- B Using codes allows more data validation checks to be carried out.
- C A hierarchical code structure makes it easier to find items on a code list, since similar items are grouped.
- D Codes in accounting reduce the need for accountants to understand the principles of accounting.

38 A firm uses a unique code to identify each customer and customer account. The code consists of the first three letters of the customer's name, followed by four digits.

Which one of the following will appear first when the customers are sorted into descending order?

- A TRO1100
- B TRO1214
- C TOP1213
- D TOR1102

39 Inventory codes used by an organisation are eight-digit numerical codes. Inventory records are held on computer in a real-time inventory control system.

Which of the following measures is most likely to prevent errors with the input of the inventory code number for each inventory transaction?

- A Existence check
- B Dual input of the inventory code
- C Verification check
- D Check digit check

40 A firm uses a unique code to identify each customer – the first four letters of each name are followed by four digits.

Which one of the following will appear first when customers are sorted into descending order?

- A ADAM0001
- B ADAA0099
- C ADDA0100
- D ABAB0999

MULTIPLE CHOICE QUESTIONS : SECTION 1

41 Which one of the following is the correct sequential flow of documents to complete the purchase of goods on credit?

- A Goods received note, purchase order, cheque requisition, invoice, delivery note
- B Purchase order, delivery note, goods received note, invoice, cheque requisition
- C Purchase order, goods received note, delivery note, cheque requisition, invoice
- D Purchase order, invoice, goods received note, cheque requisition, delivery note

42 Which member of staff is most likely to raise a goods received note?

- A Delivery driver
- B Finance director
- C Sales ledger clerk
- D Store clerk

43 Who is most likely to record deliveries into stores?

- A Stores clerk
- B Sales clerk
- C Accounts clerk
- D Personnel assistant

44 Which of the following describes a purchase order?

- A Issued by the purchasing department, sent to the supplier requesting materials.
- B Issued by the stores department, sent to the purchasing department requesting materials.
- C Received together with the materials and compared to the materials received.
- D Issued by the production department, sent to the stores department requesting materials.

COST CLASSIFICATION AND MEASUREMENT

45 Which costs are included within a prime cost?

- A All variable costs
- B Direct labour and material only
- C Direct labour, direct material and direct expense
- D Direct labour, direct material and production overhead

46 Which of the following statements best describes a semi-variable cost?

- A A cost that increases in direct proportion to output
- B A cost that remains constant irrespective of the level of output
- C A cost that contains an element of both fixed and variable cost
- D A cost that increases throughout the year

47 Which of the costs listed below is *not* a fixed cost?

- A Insurance
- B Business rates
- C Depreciation – based on straight-line method
- D Materials used in production

48 Which costs are included within production overheads?

- A Variable overheads only
- B Indirect labour, indirect material and indirect expenses related to production activity
- C Indirect expenses only
- D Indirect labour and material related to the production activity

49 Which of the following statements best describes a direct cost?

- A A cost which cannot be influenced by its budget holder
- B Expenditure which can be economically identified with a specific cost unit
- C A cost which needs to be apportioned to a cost centre
- D The highest proportion of the total cost of a product

50 What would be the most appropriate cost unit for a cake manufacturer?

- A Cake
- B Batch
- C Kilogram
- D Production run

51 A factory makes wooden chairs.

Which of the following items would be most likely to behave as stepped costs?

- A Wood used to make chairs
- B Factory supervisors' salaries
- C Heating and light costs
- D Staples to fix the fabric to the seat of the chair

52 The following graph represents which type of cost?

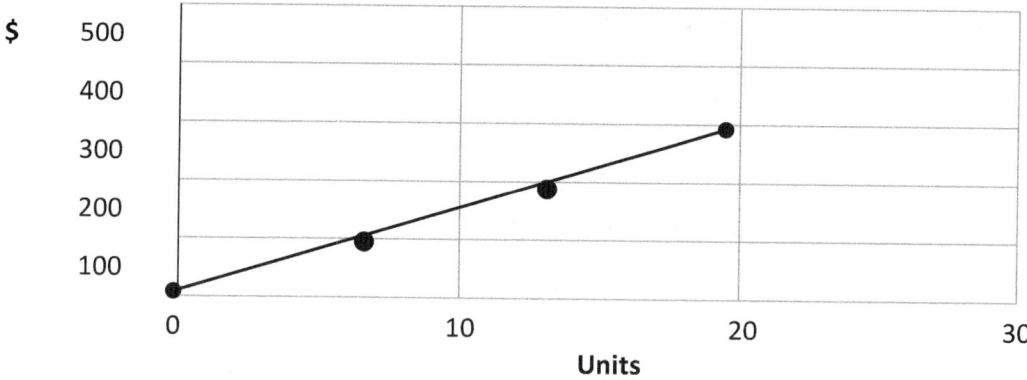

- A Fixed cost
- B Variable cost
- C Semi-variable cost
- D Stepped cost

53 For operational purposes, for a company operating a fleet of delivery vehicles, which of the following methods of calculating cost would be most useful?

- A Cost per mile run
- B Cost per driver hour
- C Cost per tonne mile
- D Cost per kilogram carried

54 The following data relate to the overhead expenditure of contract cleaners at two activity levels:

Square metres cleaned	12,750	15,100
Overheads	$73,950	$83,585

If fixed overheads are estimated to cost $21,675, what is the estimated overhead cost if 16,200 square metres are to be cleaned?

- A $66,420
- B $88,095
- C $89,674
- D $93,960

MA1 : MANAGEMENT INFORMATION

55 The following data relate to two output levels of a department:

Machine hours	17,000	18,500
Overheads	$246,500	$251,750

What is the amount of fixed overheads?

A $5,250

B $59,500

C $187,000

D $246,500

56 **Which of the following is a direct expense?**

A Materials used on production

B Special tools for job 721

C Power

D Depreciation

57 Hockey Skill manufactures hockey sticks. A summary of some cost headings include:

(a) wood used as raw material

(b) rubber covers for handles

(c) depreciation

(d) power

(e) sales manager's salary

(f) labour in assembly department

(g) oils and greases

(h) telephone and postage

(i) insurance of plant

(j) supervisory labour.

Which of the above items would be classified as production overheads?

A (a), (f), (d) and (e)

B (c), (d), (g), (i) and (j)

C (e), (h), (i) and (j)

D (a), (b), (c), (d) and (f)

58 A small engineering company that makes generators specifically to customers' own designs has had to purchase some special tools for a particular job. The tools will have no further use after the work has been completed and will be scrapped.

How should the cost of these tools be treated?

A   Variable production overheads

B   Fixed production overheads

C   Indirect expenses

D   Direct expenses

59   Which of the following statements best describes a cost centre?

A   A unit of product or service for which costs are calculated

B   An amount of profit attributable to an activity

C   A function or location within an organisation for which costs are accumulated

D   A section of the organisation for which budgets are prepared and control is exercised

60   For which of the following types of business unit would residual income be a suitable measure of performance?

A   Cost centre

B   Revenue centre

C   Profit centre

D   Investment centre

61   Which of the following is a service cost centre in a manufacturing company?

A   Finishing

B   Machining

C   Despatch

D   Assembly

62 A transport company has a cost accounting system for measuring the costs of the services it provides. The company provides train services throughout the southern region of the country.

Which of the following would be the most appropriate cost unit for measuring operating costs, in a way that costs of its various services can be usefully compared?

A   Cost per train

B   Cost per journey

C   Cost per passenger

D   Cost per passenger/kilometre

63 A training company runs courses for students that vary in length between one day and four weeks. The size of classes varies between 5 students and 40 students. The company wants to set a price for its courses based on a mark-up on cost.

What would be the most appropriate basis for measuring costs?

A   Cost per student per day

B   Cost per course

C   Cost per student

D   Cost per day

64 A law firm provides a range of services to clients, who are a mixture of business, government and private clients. It has offices in three cities in different parts of the country. The firm's senior partners are reviewing the range of services the firm provides, with a view to specialising more in the future.

How might the firm best analyse its profitability for this purpose?

A   Profitability of each office

B   Profitability of each type of service provided

C   Profitability of each type of client

D   Profitability of each employee

65 Which of the following statements is correct about costs in a manufacturing business?

A   The fixed cost per unit is the same at all levels of output

B   The fixed cost per unit falls as output increases, at a constant rate

C   The fixed cost per unit falls as output increases, at a declining rate

D   The fixed cost per unit falls as output increases, at an increasing rate

66 Which of the following is most likely to be treated as an indirect cost by a house builder?

A   Nails and screws

B   Windows

C   Bricks

D   Electricity cables

67 A travel company offers holidays to a range of destinations, which it advertises in a single brochure. Customers are transported to their destination in flights booked by the company for its exclusive use. Within each holiday destination, the company offers accommodation at different hotels, ranging from two-star to five-star hotels. The company measures the profitability of holidays to each hotel at each destination.

Which of the following would be the direct costs of a holiday at the Hotel Splendide in Trinidad?

(i) Brochure production and printing costs

(ii) Air charter flight costs

(iii) Hotel accommodation costs

A (i) and (iii) only

B (i) and (ii) only

C (ii) and (iii) only

D (iii) only

68 What is the full production cost per unit of a manufactured product?

A Direct material cost plus direct labour cost per unit

B Prime cost plus production overhead cost per unit

C Prime cost plus variable production overhead per unit

D Production overhead cost per unit

69 Which one of the following statements is true?

A Heating costs are a variable cost because they differ according to the season of the year.

B A semi-variable cost is fixed for a certain level of activity and then changes to a new fixed level.

C The fixed cost per unit of output decreases as output increases.

D Total variable costs are constant at all levels of output.

70 The following costs are recorded for different levels of production:

	Period 1	Period 2	Period 3
Costs	$1,400	$1,600	$1,600
Units of production	200	300	400

This cost could be classified as:

A fixed

B variable

C semi-variable

D stepped

71 Which of the following costs would be classified as an indirect cost?

  A   Flour for baking bread
  B   Invoice for icing a wedding cake
  C   Wages cost of baker
  D   Depreciation of ovens

72 The following charts demonstrate various costs in relation to activity:

Chart 1

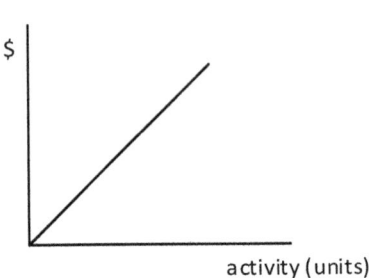
Chart 2

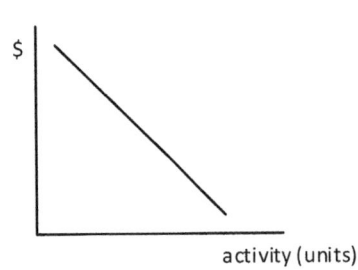
Chart 3

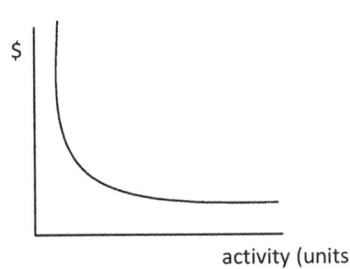
Chart 4

Which of the above charts represents variable cost per unit?

  A   Chart 1
  B   Chart 2
  C   Chart 3
  D   Chart 4

73 Which one of the following departments is *not* a service cost centre in a manufacturing company?

  A   Accounting
  B   Assembly
  C   Maintenance
  D   Personnel

74 A company operates a retail supermarket chain selling a range of grocery and household products. It has branches throughout the country and is reviewing the range of goods to be stocked in each of these branches.

How might the company best analyse its profitability for this purpose?

A   By area of the country

B   By contract with each supplier

C   By customer payment method

D   By product line stocked

75 A company produces electronic circuit boards. Each circuit board has a raw material input of $60 and labour input that costs $20. The company intends to produce 1,000 circuit boards per week. The company must also pay the rent of the factory totalling $20,000 per annum, business rates of $4,000 per annum and the production director's salary of $24,000 per annum.

What is the fixed cost of the business?

A $20,000

B $24,000

C $48,000

D $80,000

76 A large hotel has coffee shops, restaurants and banqueting. They are used by hotel residents and outside users. The manager of the hotel is responsible for encouraging residents to use the hotel's catering facilities.

Which report will show how effective the manager has been in achieving this objective?

A   A report analysing the utilisation of hotel catering services per room occupied

B   A report showing the amount of money spent in the hotel's catering facilities

C   A report showing the number of residents in the hotel at any given time

D   A report showing the occupancy of the various catering facilities

77 Which description best fits the cost curve below?

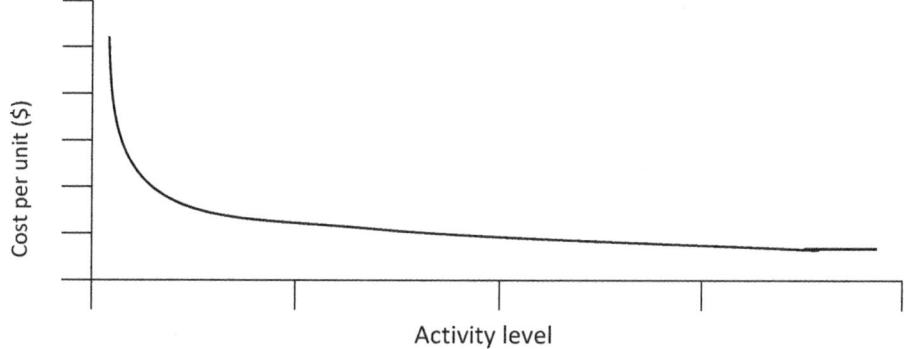

A   Direct labour cost per unit

B   Direct material cost per unit

C   Fixed production cost per unit

D   Variable production cost per unit

MA1 : MANAGEMENT INFORMATION

78 Which one of the following items is most likely to be treated as an indirect cost by a furniture manufacturer?

- A Fabric to cover the seat of a chair
- B Metal used for the legs of a chair
- C Staples to fit the fabric to the seat of a chair
- D Wood used to make the frame of a chair

79 The Rendez-Vous is a hotel, the following are either cost centres or cost units for a hotel:

- (a) Bar
- (b) Restaurant
- (c) Room/night
- (d) Meal served
- (e) Conference delegate
- (f) Fitness suite
- (g) Conference room

Which of the above items would be classified as cost units?

- A (a), (c), (d) and (f)
- B (b), (d) and (g)
- C (e), (f) and (g)
- D (c), (d) and (e)

80 Please identify the following as either cost centres or cost units for a house building company:

- (i) Quantity surveying
- (ii) Planning
- (iii) Bungalow
- (iv) Town House
- (v) Design
- (vi) Sales
- (vii) Detached House

	Cost centre	*cost unit*
A	(ii), (iii) and (iv)	(i), (v), (vi) and (vii)
B	(i), (ii), (v) and (vi)	(iii), (iv) and (vii)
C	(i), (iii) and (vii)	(ii), (iv), (v) and (vi)
D	(v), (vi) and (vii)	(i), (ii), (iii) and (iv)

81 When preparing an operating statement based on marginal costing principles, inventory valuation comprises which of the following costs?

   A   Direct labour and material only

   B   Prime cost plus production overhead

   C   Prime cost plus variable production overhead

   D   Total cost of sales

COST ACCOUNTING

82 RCW operates a bonus scheme based on time saved against a predetermined time allowance for actual output. Employees are typically expected to produce 700 units a week. The standard allowance is 20 units of 'R' per hour. In Week 6, an operative produced 750 units of 'R' in 32 hours.

   What is the time saved by this employee in Week 6 on 'R' production?

   A   2.50

   B   3.00

   C   5.50

   D   5.90

83 Gross wages incurred in a cost centre for the month of January totalled $45,250, as follows:

		$
Ordinary time	direct employees	27,500
	indirect employees	6,500
Overtime	direct employees	
	basic	4,500
	premium	2,250
Special conditions allowance	direct employees	1,300
	indirect employees	450
Shift allowance	direct employees	2,000
Sick pay	direct employees	750

   The overtime is a regular feature.

   What is the correct figure for direct wages for January?

   A $31,550

   B $32,800

   C $35,300

   D $32,000

84 HH operates an incentive scheme based on differential piecework. Employees are paid on the following basis:

Weekly output up to: 600 units   − $0.40 per unit
                        601–650 units − $0.50 per unit
                        650 units +   − $0.75 per unit

This is paid only upon production meeting quality standards with only the additional units qualifying for the higher rates. In Week 17, an employee produced 670 units, of which 10 were rejected.

What would the gross pay for the week be?

A $272.50

B $280.00

C $330.00

D $495.00

85 Which of the following methods of remuneration is NOT an incentive-based scheme?

A Straight piecework

B High day rate

C Group bonus

D Differential piecework

86 Which of the following relates to the cost of replacing (rather than retaining) labour due to high employee turnover?

A Improving working conditions

B Suffering the learning curve effect

C Provision of a pension

D Provision of welfare services

87 A job requires 2,400 actual labour hours for completion and it is anticipated that there will be 20% idle time.

If the wage rate is $10 per hour, what is the budgeted labour cost for the job?

A $19,200

B $24,000

C $28,800

D $30,000

88 A job is budgeted to require 3,300 productive hours after incurring 25% idle time.

If the total labour cost budgeted for the job is $36,300, what is the labour cost per hour?

A $8.25

B $8.80

C $11.00

D $13.75

89 **Which *one* of the following would be classified as direct labour?**

A   Personnel manager in a company servicing cars

B   Bricklayer in a construction company

C   General manager in a DIY shop

D   Maintenance manager in a company producing cameras

90 Employee A is a carpenter and normally works 36 hours per week. The standard rate of pay is $3.60 per hour. A premium of 50% of the basic hourly rate is paid for all overtime hours worked. During the last week of October 2001, Employee A worked for 42 hours. The overtime hours worked were for the following reasons:

Machine breakdown: 4 hours

To complete a special job at the request of the customer: 2 hours

How much of Employee A's earnings for the last week of October would have been treated as direct wages?

A $162.00

B $129.60

C $140.40

D $151.20

91 An employee is paid on a piecework basis. The basis of the piecework scheme is as follows:

1 to 100 units – $0.40 per unit

101 to 200 units – $0.50 per unit

201 to 299 units – $0.60 per unit

with only the additional units qualifying for the higher rates. Rejected units do not qualify for payment.

During a particular day the employee produced 240 units of which 8 were rejected as faulty.

What did the employee earn for the day's work?

A $109.20

B $114.00

C $139.20

D $144.00

MA1 : MANAGEMENT INFORMATION

92 Which of the following is usually classed as a step cost?

A Supervisor's wages

B Raw materials

C Rates

D Telephone

93 Which of the following would be most likely to provide Information on contracted rates of pay?

A a trade union

B a production manager

C a personnel manager

D a work study manager

94 Which of the following statements is correct?

A Idle time cannot be controlled because it is always due to external factors

B Idle time is always controllable because it is due to internal factors

C Idle time is always due to inefficient production staff

D Idle time is not always the fault of production staff

95 A company operates a piecework scheme to pay its staff. The staff receive $0.20 for each unit produced. However the company guarantees that every member of staff receive at least $15 per day.

Shown below is the number of units produced by Operator A during a recent week:

Day	Monday	Tuesday	Wednesday	Thursday	Friday
Units produced	90	70	75	60	90

What are Operator A's earnings for the week?

A $75.00

B $77.00

C $81.00

D $152.00

96 Which of the following statements best describes overhead allocation?

A The charging of overhead to cost units

B The allotment of proportions of items of cost to cost centres or cost units

C The charging of direct material to jobs

D The allotment of whole items of indirect cost to cost centres

97 A method of dealing with overheads involves spreading common costs over cost centres on the basis of benefit received.

What is this method known as?

- A Overhead absorption
- B Overhead apportionment
- C Overhead allocation
- D Overhead analysis

98 Production supervisory salaries are classed as production overhead.

Which is the most appropriate basis of apportioning this cost to cost centres?

- A Number of units produced
- B Machine hours
- C Direct labour hours
- D Number of machines

99 **Which of the following would be the most appropriate basis for apportioning machinery insurance costs to cost centres within a factory?**

- A The number of machines in each cost centre
- B The floor area occupied by the machinery in each cost centre
- C The value of the machinery in each cost centre
- D The operating hours of the machinery in each cost centre

100 **Factory overheads can be absorbed by which of the following methods?**

1 Direct labour hours
2 Machine hours
3 Indirect labour hours
4 $x per unit

- A 1, 2, 3 or 4
- B 1 and 2 only
- C 1, 2 or 4 only
- D 2, 3 or 4 only

MA1 : MANAGEMENT INFORMATION

101 A business employs two grades of labour in its production department. Grade A workers are considered direct labour employees, and are paid $10 per hour. Grade B workers are considered indirect labour employees, and are paid $6 per hour.

In the week just ended, Grade A labour worked 30 hours of overtime, 10 hours on a specific customer order at the customer's request, and the other 20 hours as general overtime. Grade B labour worked 45 hours of overtime, as general overtime. Overtime is paid at time-and-one-half.

What would be the total amount of pay for overtime worked in the week that is considered to be a direct labour cost?

- A $50
- B $150
- C $285
- D $350

102 A manufacturing business is currently extremely busy and overtime is being worked.

How would the cost of the overtime premium payable to direct labour employees normally be treated?

- A a direct cost
- B a production overhead cost
- C an administration overhead cost
- D a prime cost

103 Which one of the following would be classed as indirect labour?

- A Assembly workers in a firm that manufactures digital video recorders
- B A stores assistant in a factory stores
- C A plasterer in a building construction firm
- D An audit clerk in a firm of auditors

104 What is cost apportionment?

- A Charging discrete, identifiable items of cost to cost centres or cost units.
- B The collection of costs attributable to cost centres and cost units using the costing methods applied by the business.
- C The process of establishing the costs of cost centres or cost units.
- D The division of a cost between two or more cost centres in proportion to the estimated benefit received by each centre.

105 A manufacturer employs two grades of labour in its machining department, grade A and grade B. Grade A employees are treated as direct labour employees and grade B employees are treated as indirect labour employees. Grade A employees are paid $8 per hour and grade B workers receive $6 per hour. The basic working week is 40 hours. Overtime is paid at time + 50%, to all employees in the department. There are 10 grade A employees and 6 grade B employees.

During a particular week, each grade A employee worked for 45 hours and each grade B employee worked for 43 hours. The overtime was necessary due to staff sickness.

What will be the charge to production overhead for the week?

A $54

B $254

C $1,602

D $1,802

106 The payroll department has produced the following information for the month about the pay for employees in department X.

Department X	$
Payments to employees	7,500
Income tax	2,500
Employees' state benefit contributions (NI in the UK)	1,200
Employer's state benefit contributions (NI in the UK)	2,000

What are the gross wages for the department for the month?

A $7,500

B $10,000

C $11,200

D $13,200

107 The payroll department has produced the following information for the month about the pay for employees in department Z. Department Z is a part of the accounts division.

Department Z	$
Salaries (gross wages)	23,000
Income tax	4,500
Employees' state benefit contributions (NI in the UK)	2,400
Employer's state benefit contributions (NI in the UK)	3,500

What is the labour cost in Department Z that would be treated as administration overhead cost for the month?

A $23,000

B $26,500

C $29,900

D $33,400

108 An employee is paid on a stepped piecework basis, as follows:

Units produced each week	$
1 – 200	0.60 per unit
201 – 300	0.80 per unit
Over 301	1.00 per unit

Only the additional units qualify for the higher rates. Rejected units do not qualify for any payment

During a particular week, the employee makes 380 units, of which 35 were rejected as faulty.

What were his gross earnings for the week?

- A $245
- B $280
- C $345
- D $380

109 What would be the appropriate basis for apportioning the costs of heating and lighting between cost centres in a factory building?

- A Number of employees
- B Number of machines
- C Value of machinery
- D Floor area occupied by each department

110 What would be the appropriate basis for apportioning the factory manager's salary between cost centres in a factory building?

- A Number of employees
- B Number of machines
- C Value of machinery
- D Floor area occupied by each department

111 A business maintains an inventory control database. For each item of inventory, the file contains the quantity of free inventory for the item. For inventory item 245711, the current quantity held by the business is 400 units. The stores department has received requisitions from user departments for 320 units, which have yet to be processed and dealt with. An order for a new supply of 350 units has been placed with the supplier, and delivery is expected in one or two days.

What is the quantity of free inventory for this item?

- A 30
- B 370
- C 400
- D 430

112 A company employs 20 direct production operatives and 10 indirect staff in its manufacturing department. The normal operating hours for all employees is 38 hours per week and all staff are paid a basic rate of $5 per hour. Overtime hours are paid at the basic rate + 50%. During a particular week all employees worked for 44 hours to meet the company's general production requirements.

What amount would be charged to production overhead?

- A $300
- B $450
- C $2,350
- D $2,650

113 With which costs is absorption costing concerned?

- A   Direct labour costs only
- B   Direct material costs only
- C   Fixed costs only
- D   Variable and fixed costs

114 Aspects of payroll include:

1   Employer's state benefit contribution (National Insurance in the UK)
2   Employee's state benefit contribution (National Insurance in the UK)
3   Income tax (PAYE in the UK)
4   Salaries

Which of the above are costs to an employer?

- A   1 and 4 only
- B   2 and 4 only
- C   2, 3 and 4 only
- D   1, 2, 3 and 4

115 An employee is paid on a piecework basis. The scheme is as follows:

1 – 100 units per day	$0.20 per unit
101 – 200 units per day	$0.30 per unit
> 200 units per day	$0.40 per unit

Only the additional units qualify for the higher rates. Rejected units do not qualify for payment. An employee produced 210 units in a day of which 17 were rejected as faulty.

How much did the employee earn for the day?

- A $47.90
- B $54.00
- C $57.90
- D $84.00

116 It is possible for an item of overhead expenditure to be shared amongst several cost centres. It is also possible that an item of overhead expenditure may relate to just one specific cost centre.

What term is used to describe charging an item of overhead to just one specific cost centre?

A Absorption

B Allocation

C Apportionment

D Re-apportionment

117 What would be the most appropriate basis for apportioning machinery insurance costs to cost centres within a factory?

A Floor area occupied by the machinery

B Number of machines

C Operating hours of machinery

D Value of machinery

118 There are 275 units of material BX in stock. An order for 650 units is expected and a material requisition for 300 units has not yet been issued to the production cost centre.

What is the free inventory?

A 275 units

B 625 units

C 650 units

D 675 units

119 A company employs 30 direct production staff and 15 indirect staff in its manufacturing department. The normal operating hours for all employees is 37 hours per week and all staff are paid a basic rate of $8 per hour. Overtime hours are paid at the basic rate + 50%. During a particular week all employees worked for 42 hours to meet the company's general production requirements.

What is the total direct labour cost?

A $8,880

B $10,080

C $10,680

D $10,980

120 An employee is paid on a piecework basis. The scheme is as follows:

1 – 200 units per day $0.15 per unit
201 – 500 units per day $0.20 per unit
> 500 units per day $0.25 per unit

Only the additional units qualify for the higher rates. Rejected units do not qualify for payment. An employee produced 512 units in a day of which 17 were rejected as faulty.

What wage is paid to the employee?

A $128
B $103
C $99
D $89

121 It is expected that a product will take 36 minutes to produce. In a period 180 hours are worked and 325 units of product are made. A bonus of half of the time saved is paid to the employees. The wage rate is $8.00 per hour.

What is the total amount of bonus paid to the employees?

A $252
B $120
C $60
D   None

122 In a payments by results scheme employees are paid a bonus based on hours saved at the basic wage rate. The bonus payable to the employee is calculated as the hours saved multiplied by the ratio of time saved to time allowed.

An employee produces 480 units in 72 hours. The time allowed for this number of units is 108 hours. The employee's basic rate of pay is $10 per hour.

What is the total amount payable to the employee for this job?

A $120
B $720
C $733
D $840

123 A company operates a job costing system. Job 812 requires $60 of direct materials, $40 of direct labour and $20 of direct expenses. Direct labour is paid $8 per hour. Production overheads are absorbed at a rate of $16 per direct labour hour and non-production overheads are absorbed at a rate of 60% of prime cost.

What is the total cost of Job 812?

A $240
B $260
C $272
D $320

MA1 : MANAGEMENT INFORMATION

124 Which one of the following statements is incorrect?

A   Job costs are collected separately, whereas process costs are averages

B   In job costing the progress of a job can be ascertained from the materials requisition notes and job tickets or time sheet

C   In process costing information is needed about work passing through a process and work remaining in each process

D   In process costing, but not job costing, the cost of normal loss will be incorporated into normal product costs

125 A firm uses job costing and recovers overheads on a direct labour cost basis.

Two jobs were worked on during a period, the details of which were:

	Job 1 $	Job 2 $	Job 3 $
Opening work-in-progress	8,500	0	32,000
Material in period	17,150	29,025	5,675
Labour for period	12,500	23,000	4,500

The overheads for the period were exactly as budgeted, $140,000. Actual labour costs were also the same as budgeted.

Jobs 1 and 2 were the only incomplete jobs at the end of the period.

What was the value of closing work-in-progress?

A $81,900

B $90,175

C $140,675

D $214,425

126 A firm uses job costing and recovers overheads at a rate of 350% of the direct labour cost.

Job 352 was completed during the period and consisted of 2,400 identical circuit boards. The firm adds 50% to total production costs to arrive at a selling price.

The details of job 352 were:	$
Opening work-in-progress	46,000
Material in period	0
Labour for period	4,500

What is the selling price of a circuit board?

A   It cannot be calculated without more information

B $31.56

C $41.41

D $58.33

127 A company uses process costing to value its output. The following was recorded for the period:

Input materials   2,000 units at $4.50 per unit
Conversion costs $13,040
Loss   5% of input

There were no opening or closing inventories.

What was the valuation of one unit of output?

A $11.80
B $11.60
C $11.20
D $11.00

128 In a production process the percentage completion of the work-in-progress (WIP) at the end of a period is found to have been understated.

When this is corrected what will be the effect on the cost per unit and the total value of the WIP?

	Cost per unit	Total value of WIP
A	Decrease	Decrease
B	Decrease	Increase
C	Increase	Decrease
D	Increase	Increase

129 The direct costs for batch number 35401, comprising 200 men's shirts, were as follows:

Materials $3,000
Labour   120 hours @$5 per hour

Production overheads are absorbed at a company-wide rate of $12 per direct labour hour.

Non-production overheads are absorbed at the rate of $1,000 per batch.

What is the total production cost per unit of each shirt in the batch?

A $18.00
B $22.20
C $25.20
D $30.20

130 C $1.28

131 D $20.00

132 D $10.00

133 A small management consultancy has prepared the following information:

Overhead absorption rate per consulting hour $12.50
Salary cost per consulting hour (senior) $20.00
Salary cost per consulting hour (junior) $15.00

The firm adds 40% to total cost to arrive at a selling price.

Assignment number 652 took 86 hours of a senior consultant's time and 220 hours of a junior consultant's time.

What price should be charged for assignment 652?

A $5,355
B $7,028
C $8,845
D $12,383

134 In the context of process costing, which of the following best describes an 'equivalent unit'?

A a unit of cost based on optimum efficiency
B an effective whole unit representing the varying degrees of completion of work
C a unit made in more than one process cost centre.
D a unit being currently made which is the same as previously manufactured

The following information relates to questions 135 to 137.

The inventory record for component BXY for the month of January showed:

	Receipts	Value $	Issues
Opening inventory	500	1,250	
4 January	1,000	2,750	
11 January	1,600	4,480	
18 January	1,200	3,480	
19 January			2,100
25 January	1,500	4,350	
31 January			1,800

135 Using the FIFO method of pricing issues, the cost of issues during the month was:

A $11,250
B $10,800
C $10,850
D $11,300

MA1 : MANAGEMENT INFORMATION

136 Using the LIFO method of pricing issues, what is the value of inventory at 31 January?

    A $4,100

    B $3,720

    C $5,120

    D $3,950

137 Using the AVCO method of pricing, at what price would the issues on 31 January be made?

(Calculate to two decimal places.)

    A $3.00

    B $2.95

    C $2.90

    D $2.83

The following information relates to questions 138 and 139.

Turner has the following inventory record:

Date		Number of units	Cost
1 March	Opening inventory	100 units	at $3.00/unit
3 March	Receipt	200 units	at $3.50/unit
8 March	Issue	250 units	
15 March	Receipt	300 units	at $3.20/unit
17 March	Receipt	200 units	at $3.30/unit
21 March	Issue	500 units	
23 March	Receipt	450 units	at $3.10/unit
27 March	Issue	350 units	

138 What is the valuation of closing inventory if LIFO is used?

    A $460

    B $465

    C $467

    D $469

139 What is the valuation of issues using the weighted average method of inventory valuation at each issue?

    A $3,248

    B $3,548

    C $3,715

    D $4,015

The following information relates to questions 140 and 141.

Date		Units	Unit price ($)	Value ($)
1 Jan 20X1	Balance b/f	100	5.00	500.00
3 Mar 20X1	Issue	40		
4 Jun 20X1	Receipt	50	5.50	275.00
6 Jun 20X1	Receipt	50	6.00	300.00
9 SEP 20X1	**ISSUE**	**70**		

140 If the first-in, first-out method of pricing had been used the value of the issue on 9 September 20X1 would have been:

    A $350

    B $355

    C $395

    D $420

141 If the last-in, first-out method of pricing had been used the value of the issue on 9 September 20X1 would have been:

    A $350

    B $395

    C $410

    D $420

142 A company uses the first-in, first-out (FIFO) method to price issues of raw material to production and to value its closing inventory.

Which of the following statements best describes the first-in, first-out method?

    A   The last materials received will be the first issued to production

    B   The first materials issued will be priced at the cost of the most recently received materials

    C   The last materials issued will be those that were most recently received

    D   The first materials issued will be priced at the cost of the earliest goods still in inventory

143 If a company is using the first-in, first-out method for material issues at a time when material prices are rising this will mean which of the following?

    A   Production costs will be lower and profits will be higher than if the last-in, first-out method had been used

    B   Production costs will be higher and profits will be lower than if the last-in, first-out method had been used

    C   Production costs will be lower and profits will be lower than if the last-in, first-out method had been used

    D   Production costs will be higher and profits will be higher than if the last-in, first-out method had been used

MA1 : MANAGEMENT INFORMATION

144 A manufacturer holds inventory of a raw material item. The manufacturer makes and sells a single product, and each unit of product uses 2.5 kilograms of the raw material. The budgeted production for the year is 6000 units of the product. At the start of the year, the manufacturer expects to have 1800 kg of the raw material item in inventory, but plans to reduce inventory levels by one-third by the end of the year.

What will be the budgeted purchase quantities of the raw material item in the year?

A 13,800 kg

B 14,400 kg

C 15,000 kg

D 15,600 kg

145 A manufacturing company has budgeted sales next year of 5,000 units of product T. Each unit of product T uses 3 units of a component X. The company plans to increase inventory levels of finished goods by 200 units by the end of the year, and to increase inventory levels of component X by 400 units.

What will be the budgeted purchase quantities of component X for the year?

A 15,200 units

B 15,400 units

C 15,600 units

D 16,000 units

146 A manufacturing company makes and sells a single product. The sales budget for the year is 8,000 units. Each unit of the product requires 1.2 kilograms of raw materials. The company has budgeted to reduce inventory levels of finished goods from 2,000 units at the start of the year to 1,500 units at the end of the year, but it plans to increase inventory levels of the raw material from 1,500 kilograms to 2,400 kilograms.

What will be the budgeted purchase quantities of raw materials for the year?

A 8,100 kilograms

B 8,300 kilograms

C 9,900 kilograms

D 10,200 kilograms

THE SPREADSHEET SYSTEM

147 In the Excel spreadsheet below, what is the name given to cell B6?

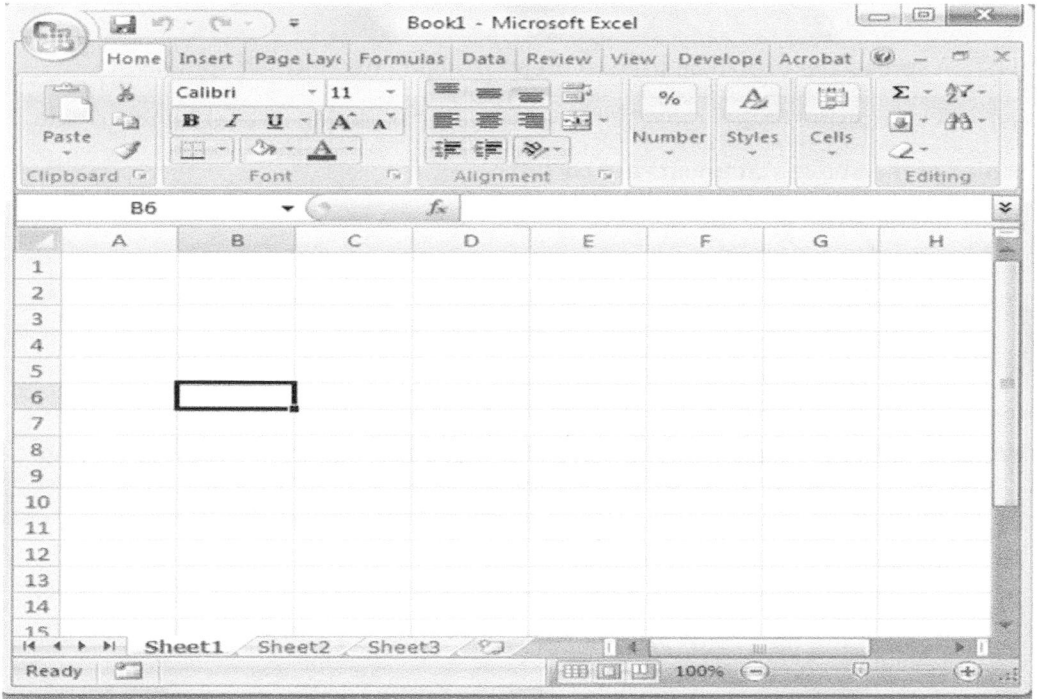

A work cell

B current cell

C active cell

D key cell

148 You prepare a budget using a spreadsheet program. The numerical data is presented in a tabular form. However, the tabulated data can also be presented in alternative or additional forms.

Which of the following methods of data presentation *cannot* be produced automatically by a spreadsheet program?

A Bar chart

B Narrative (words)

C Pie chart

D Graph

MA1 : MANAGEMENT INFORMATION

149 The following statements relate to spreadsheets:

(i) A spreadsheet consists of records and files.

(ii) Most spreadsheets have a facility to allow data within them to be displayed graphically.

(iii) A spreadsheet could be used to prepare a budgeted income statement.

(iv) A spreadsheet is the most suitable software for storing large volumes of data.

Which of the above statements are correct?

A (i) and (ii) only

B (i), (iii) and (iv) only

C (ii) and (iii) only

D (iii) and (iv) only

150 Which of the following are advantages of spreadsheet software over manual approaches?

(i) Security

(ii) Speed

(iii) Accuracy

(iv) Legibility

A All of them

B (ii), (iii) and (iv)

C (ii) and (iv)

D (i) and (iv)

151 A company manufactures a single product. In a computer spreadsheet the cells F1 to F12 contain the budgeted monthly sales units for the 12 months of next year in sequence with January sales in cell F1 and finishing with December sales in F12. The company policy is for the closing inventory of finished goods each month to be 10% of the budgeted sales units for the following month.

Which of the following formulae will generate the budgeted production (in units) for March next year?

A =[F3 +(0.1*F4)]

B =[F3 -(0.1*F4)]

C =[(1.1*F3) - (0.1*F4)]

D =[(0.9*F3) +(0.1*F4)]

152 Which of the following is not one of the main aspects of formatting cells?

A Wrapping text

B Using graphics

C Setting number specification, e.g. working to 2 decimal places

D Changing the font, size or colour of text

MULTIPLE CHOICE QUESTIONS : SECTION 1

153 For which of the following tasks would a spreadsheet be most useful?

- A   Exception reporting
- B   Annual staff appraisals
- C   Writing a news letter
- D   Categorising products by a range of different factors (price, location, customer, date launched, etc)

154 The following spreadsheet shows an extract from a company's cash flow forecast.

	A	B	C	D	E
1	Cash flow forecast				
2					
3			Jan	Feb	March
4	Inflows				
5	Cash sales		10,000	12,000	11,500
6	Cash from debtors		24,500	26,200	15,630
7	Disposal of non-current assets		0	0	12,000
8	Other		10	0	0
9	Total inflows		34,510	38,200	39,130

Which of the following formulae will generate the correct figure for cell D9?

- A   SUM(D5:D8)
- B   SUM(D5;D8)
- C   =SUM(D5:D8)
- D   =SUM(D5;D8)

155 Figures in a spreadsheet cell have been formatted as 'number'.

Which of the following characteristics will NOT be available to adjust?

- A   Number of decimal places
- B   Commas to indicate thousands
- C   Negative number formatting options
- D   Currency symbols

156 Figures in a spreadsheet cell have been formatted as 'accounting'.

Which of the following characteristics will NOT be available to adjust?

- A   Number of decimal places
- B   Commas to indicate thousands
- C   Negative number formatting options
- D   Currency symbols

MA1 : MANAGEMENT INFORMATION

157 **What is the effect of using brackets in a spreadsheet formula?**

    A   Divisions and multiplications are calculated before additions and subtractions

    B   Additions and subtractions are calculated before divisions and multiplications

    C   The contents of the brackets are calculated first

    D   The contents of the brackets are calculated last

158 The following spreadsheet shows an extract from a company's sales figures.

	A	B	C	D	E
1	Sales				
2					
3			2010	2011	2012
4	Region				
5	NW		10,000	12,000	11,500
6	NE		7,000	6,200	8,200
7	SE		3,000	10,000	12,000
8	SW		1,500	5,750	5,600

The management accountant wishes to produce a chart to demonstrate the trends over time between the different regions and is considering the following charts:

(i)   Stacked (compound) bar chart

(ii)   Line charts

(iii)   Pie charts

Which of the charts would be effective at demonstrating the trends?

    A   (i) only

    B   (i) and (ii)

    C   (ii) only

    D   (i), (ii) and (iii)

159 **What type of error message does Excel give when you try to divide by a blank cell?**

    A   #VALUE!

    B   #DIV/0!

    C   #NUM!

    D   #REF!

160 **What type of error message does Excel give when you place an invalid argument in a function?**

    A   #VALUE!

    B   #DIV/0!

    C   #NUM!

    D   #REF!

161 Which of the following are correct descriptions applied to computer spreadsheets?

(1) The intersection of each row and column defines a cell
(2) Data is organised in rows and columns
(3) An entire page of rows and columns is called a workbook
(4) Each column is identified by a number

A (1) and (2) only
B (2) and (4) only
C (3) and (4) only
D (1), (2), (3) and (4)

162 Which of the following statements concerning spreadsheet cells are correct?

(1) A formula in a particular cell may calculate numbers for several cells
(2) Pressing CONTROL and END takes you to the last cell you entered anything into
(3) Each cell can contain text, a number or a formula
(4) Pressing CONTROL and HOME takes you to cell A1

A (1), (2) and (4)
B (1), (3) and (4)
C (2) and (3) only
D (3) and (4) only

163 Which of the following are reasons for formatting data in a spreadsheet?

(1) To make text (i.e. labels) more visually interesting
(2) To get data into the correct order for analysis
(3) To make numbers more descriptive of what they represent
(4) To make the data appear as plain text

A (1) and (3) only
B (2) and (3) only
C (2) and (4) only
D (1), (2) and (3)

164 Wrap text is an important formatting function which:

A Places a border around the highlighted text
B Increase the height of a row containing text so that the whole of the text is visible
C Aligns the text to the left, right or centre
D Changes the size and font of the text

MA1 : MANAGEMENT INFORMATION

165 What is the default printing option in Excel?

- A Portrait, A4 with gridlines
- B Landscape, A4 without gridlines
- C Portrait, A4 without gridlines
- D Landscape, A4 with gridlines

166 What would be the most effective way of demonstrating a trend in new mobile telephone sales from January to December 20X1?

- A Pie chart
- B Bar chart
- C Table
- D Line graph

167 You work in the accounts department of a company. Your friend in the sales department has requested some accounting information and assures you that the finance director is aware of this request.

Which ONE of the following should you do?

- A Print out the information and give it to them
- B Give them your computer password and let them use your computer
- C Decline the request
- D Confirm the request with the finance director

168 Which of the following keyboard shortcuts in Excel will print the spreadsheet you have produced?

- A Ctrl + C > OK
- B Ctrl + P > OK
- C Ctrl + F > OK
- D Ctrl + R > OK

169 On an Excel spreadsheet, a value is typed in to a cell as '10.567'. The cell is formatted as 'Number, General'.

How will the number appear in the cell?

- A 10.5
- B 10.567
- C $10.567
- D ########

170 In 'Format cells, Number, Percentage', the figure 0.25 will be shown in a cell as:

- A   0.25
- B   0.25%
- C   25.00
- D   25.00%

171 If cell B3 contains the value 10.567 and cell B4 contains the formula '=ROUND(B3,0)', the value contained in cell B4 would be:

- A   11
- B   10.6
- C   10.57
- D   10.567

172 To make a cell address absolute .i.e. to always use the contents of that cell, which ONE of the following symbols should be used?

- A   £
- B $
- C   %
- D   *

173 A salesman receives a basic salary and a bonus based on 5% of sales made. His basic salary is entered on to a spreadsheet in cell B5. His sales figure is split between 'home' sales in cell C5 and 'overseas' sales in cell D5. The commission percentage of 5% is entered in cell E5. Total commission is calculated in cell F5 and would be determined using the formula:

- A   =(C5 + D5)*E5
- B   C5+D5*E5
- C   (C5+D5)*E5
- D   =C5+D5*E5

174 In cell B2 an accountant enters the number of hours employees usually work per week, which is 40 hours. In cells C10 to C14 the employees' actual hours worked are entered. They range from 38 to 42 hours dependent on the employee. In cells D10 to D14 the accountant wishes to note whether the employee will receive overtime, by using an IF function. Cell D10 should hold the formula:

- A   =IF(C$10>B2,'OVERTIME','N/A')
- B   =IF($C$10>B2,'OVERTIME','N/A')
- C   =IF(C10>$B2,'OVERTIME','N/A')
- D   =IF(C10>$B$2,'OVERTIME','N/A')

175 The data below is not arranged in any order.

	A	B	C	D	E
1	Supplier	Quantity	Price($)	Value($)	Rank
2	X	10	2	20	
3	Z	124		48	
4	W	115		55	
5	Y	133		39	

To SORT the Price ($) into descending order you should start by:

A Selecting the data range A2:C5> Data> Sort, Choose to sort Column C

B Selecting the data range A2:C5> Data, Choose to sort Column C> Sort

C Selecting the data range C2:C5> Data> Sort> Choose to sort Column C

D Selecting the data range C2:C5> Sort> Data, Choose to sort Column C

176 A company manufactures three products and wants to show how the sales mix of each product has changed from 20X1 to 20X8. Which of the following charts or diagrams would be most suitable for showing this information?

A Pie chart

B Component bar chart

C Simple bar chart

D Line graph

177 XYZ sells into ten different countries. Which would be the most appropriate chart or diagram for showing total turnover for the year and its split into different countries?

A Simple bar chart

B Line graph

C Pie chart

D Scatter diagram

178 Non-financial managers are likely to experience problems in understanding and interpreting management accounting reports.

Which of the following statements is the *least* appropriate method of dealing with this problem?

A Highlight and explain any unusual items in the report

B Discuss with users the most appropriate form of report

C Include clear graphics and charts, and ensure that the narrative is as simple as possible

D Ensure that only individuals with some accounting knowledge are appointed to management positions

179 Three dimensional spreadsheet would be best described by which of the following?

- A   Spreadsheets which need special glasses for users to be able to read them
- B   Spreadsheets which need an extra, 3D programme to make them viewable on a normal computer screen
- C   Spreadsheets which use a number of worksheets, each one linked to an overall summary worksheet
- D   Spreadsheets spread over a number of workbooks which are not linked together

180 Which of the following are justifications for the widespread use of computers in the provision of management information?

1   Speed of processing
2   Accuracy of processing
3   Volume and complexity of processing requirements

- A   1 and 2 only
- B   1 and 3 only
- C   2 and 3 only
- D   1, 2 and 3

181 Which of the following is the correct syntax for a ROUND function?

- A   Round(number,digits)
- B   Round(digits,number)
- C   Round(number,digits,0)
- D   Round(digits,number,0)

182 Which of the following is least likely to be prepared using a spreadsheet?

- A   Variance reports
- B   Annual accounts
- C   Cash forecast
- D   Annual budget

183 Which of the following mathematical symbols used in formulae is in the correct order of precedence in spreadsheet calculations?

- A   ^ / + -
- B   + - / ^
- C   + - ^ /
- D   / ^ + -

184 If three adjacent columns are selected at once and the hide function is used, which column or columns will be hidden?

- A   All three columns
- B   The column in the middle only
- C   The columns on the outside only
- D   No columns

185 To unhide a hidden row, a user must first select?

- A   The row that is hidden
- B   The rows above and below the hidden row
- C   The entire worksheet
- D   The entire workbook

186 Which of the following password options would allow a user to view a spreadsheet but not allow them to make changes without entering a password?

- A   Password to open
- B   Password to modify
- C   Read only recommended
- D   None of the above

187 When protecting individual cells in a spreadsheet, what must a user do to the worksheet?

- A   Lock the worksheet
- B   Protect the worksheet
- C   Unprotect the worksheet
- D   Nothing at all

188 Which of the following custom formats would result in negative numbers being shown with brackets around them?

- A   -#,##0
- B   #,##0,(#,##0)
- C   #,##0;-#,##0
- D   #,##0;(#,##0)

189 Which of the following custom formats would result in numbers with a zero value not being displayed on a spreadsheet?

- A   -#,##0;
- B   #,##0;(#,##0);0
- C   #,##0;[Zero]
- D   #,##0;(#,##0);

190 How should the time 25 past four p.m. be entered onto a spreadsheet?

- A   16.25.00 pm
- B   4;25;00 pm
- C   16:25:00
- D   16;25;00

191 Examine the following spreadsheet extract:

	A	B	C	D
1	Sales Month	Product 1	Product 2	Total
2	Jan	15	8	23
3	Feb	16	7	23
4	Mar	14	Four	
5				

The formula in cell D2 is: =B2+C2.

If this formula was copied to cell D4, which error message would appear?

- A   #DIV/0!
- B   #VALUE!
- C   #REF!
- D   #NAME?

192 Which of the following is not an advantage of component bar charts?

- A   The relative importance of each component can be assessed
- B   The information can be interpreted quickly
- C   More than one component can be displayed at a time
- D   The total value can be easily assessed and determined

193 Which of the following graphs would best be used to identify trends in data?

- A   A bar chart
- B   A pie chart
- C   A line graph
- D   A scatter graph

194 Which of the following graphs would best be used to illustrate that two variables are uncorrelated?

- A   A bar chart
- B   A pie chart
- C   A line graph
- D   A scatter graph

MA1 : MANAGEMENT INFORMATION

195 Under which menu is the chart wizard found in Microsoft Excel 2010?

- A Formulas
- B Page Layout
- C View
- D Insert

196 Which of the following chart options would allow a user to change the positioning of the key which explains what each bar represents in a bar chart?

- A Chart title
- B Legend
- C Data labels
- D Data table

197 Which of the following is the best way to ensure that the titles on a spreadsheet remain in view regardless of which position a user scrolls to within the spreadsheet?

- A Split screen
- B Freeze panes
- C Consolidate data
- D Rename the columns

198 Which of the following allows a user to determine which part of a spreadsheet is printed?

- A Page setup
- B Margins setup
- C Header/footer settings
- D Sheet setup

199 Which of the following allows a user to access more worksheets than the standard three?

- A Press 'Shift' and 'F11'
- B Press 'File', 'Worksheet', '4'
- C Press 'Shift', 'F10'
- D Press 'File', 'Worksheet'

200 Which of the following functions allows a user to locate the word 'January' in their spreadsheet and change it to the word 'February'?

- A Find and replace
- B Find and select
- C Locate and replace
- D Locate and select

MULTIPLE CHOICE QUESTIONS : SECTION 1

201 Which of the following allows a user to save their spreadsheet?

- A   Click on 'File', 'Save As'
- B   Right click the mouse and select Save
- C   Left click on the mouse and press Save
- D   Click on 'Save'

202 Which of the following would indicate that a comment has been added to a cell?

- A   A red marker in the top left of the cell
- B   A red marker in the top right of the cell
- C   A blue marker in the top left of the cell
- D   A blue marker in the top right of the cell

Section 2

ANSWERS TO MULTIPLE CHOICE QUESTIONS

THE NATURE AND PURPOSE OF COST AND MANAGEMENT ACCOUNTING

1 C

With an integrated accounting system, the same ledger is used for accounts to prepare both financial accounting and management accounting information. As a consequence, transactions entered into the system need to be coded for both financial accounting and management accounting purposes. Individual ledger accounts for receivables and payables are needed in an accounting system, including an integrated accounts system.

2 D

Information needs to be timely – i.e. available in time for when it is needed. This is not necessarily the same as having the information available quickly, although with on-line Internet connections, it is increasingly common for information to be needed quickly.

3 D

Data consists of numbers, letters, symbols, raw facts, events and transactions which have been recorded but not yet processed into a form which is suitable for making decisions. Information is data which has been processed in such a way that it has a meaning to the person who receives it, who may then use it to improve the quality of decision making.

4 D

All four answers are purposes of information, but providing information to customers is an example of information for an external third party, rather than *management* information.

5 A

Cost accounting can be used for inventory valuation to meet the requirements of both internal reporting and external financial reporting.

MA1 : MANAGEMENT INFORMATION

6   B

Information should have certain qualities. These do not include being in either digital or printed format, nor does information have to be universal (whatever 'universal' means). Some qualities are sometimes desirable in information, such as brevity and being secure (if the information is confidential). Only answer B includes three qualities of good information, reliability, consistency and being available in time to be used (timeliness).

7   A

Financial accounting reports are prepared for external users, such as shareholders and the tax authorities, whereas management accounting reports are produced for use by management. Management accounting reports should be frequent and should contain the details that management require. However, the information in both management accounting reports and financial accounting statements should be accurate.

8   C

Information should always be reliable, otherwise it is of doubtful value. Not all information needs to be available immediately. Confidential information must not be available to everyone. Information only needs to be technically accurate if technical accuracy is required for its purpose.

9   B

Information is processed data. The distinction is that data is unprocessed whereas information is processed.

10   D

Items A, B and C should all be available from the financial accounting system. Cost and management accounting is more concerned with analysing the costs and profitability of products, services, activities and decisions, and with producing information for planning and control by management.

11   A

External information is obtained from sources outside the organisation. Statistics relating to the consumer price index come from the government. Information about price lists, production volumes and discounts to customers comes from sources within the organisation.

12   C

Management accounting is concerned with providing information to management to help them with planning, control and decision making. A budget (plan) for future sales, a variance report comparing actual results with a budget, and profitability reports are therefore all management accounting reports. Payroll is a separate activity. Management accounts would make use of total labour costs from the payroll system, but a payroll report is not a management accounting report.

ANSWERS TO MULTIPLE CHOICE QUESTIONS : SECTION 2

13   C

Management accounts record revenues and costs. Sales commissions are a sales overhead cost and repairs to the office air conditioning system are an administration overhead cost. Dividends paid to the business owners are relevant to the financial accounts, not the management accounts.

14   B

Information cannot make sure that managers take the correct or best decision every time. It should give managers a better understanding, however, that should help them to reach a more informed decision. As a consequence, in the long term, the quality of management decision making should be much better. Answer C is not correct: allocating blame after the event is not a primary aspect of decision making.

15   A

Office manuals cover all predictable and routine operations and procedures, rather than unusual and out-of-the-ordinary cases. However, they can be used for reference or checking in cases of doubt. They are also used for the induction and training of staff. They also establish the methods for getting work done, and so they can be helpful in maintaining performance standards, provided staff are aware of what they contain.

16   C

'Prime' means 'first', and prime entry records are the first records of transactions entered in the accounting system. They are recorded in books of prime entry for convenience. Subsequently, the transactions are transferred to ('posted' to) the ledger accounts.

17   D

Statement 1 is incorrect. In a system of interlocking accounts, financial accounts and management accounts are recorded in different ledgers. Statement 2 is correct: errors will be less in a computerised system partly because of validation checks on input that can be carried out by a computer program and partly because transactions are only entered once and posting transactions to the ledgers is done automatically, reducing the likelihood of error. Statement 3 is also correct: transactions should be recorded more quickly because they are entered once into the system, and subsequent postings and transfers to the ledgers are done automatically.

18   C

Double entry bookkeeping is a system of recording transactions relating to income, expenditure, assets, liabilities and capital twice in the main ledger (often called the nominal ledger or general ledger). The transaction is recorded as a 'debit' entry in one account in the ledger and also as a 'credit' entry in another account in the same ledger. Answer A is incorrect: computer systems as well as manual systems are based on double entry bookkeeping principles. Answer B is not an accurate definition, and answer D is totally incorrect.

19   A

All of the others have been processed in some way and are information.

MA1 : MANAGEMENT INFORMATION

20 C

Primary data is data which is used solely for the purpose for which it was collected.

21 B

Limited companies are required by law to prepare financial statements.

22 B

This is an unsatisfactory question. Answers A and C are not correct, because they describe activities. Statistics (answer D) are specifically numerical data/information, whereas facts and information can be non-numerical. Answer B is the required answer, although it is not strictly correct to describe information as 'data'. Information is processed data.

23 D

Management information and operating information are not the same, and there is no requirement for management information to be produced by computer. (Answers A and B are incorrect.) Complete accuracy is not necessarily a desirable quality of information, especially if it costs a lot to obtain the perfect degree of accuracy (so answer C is incorrect). Management information is desirable if the cost of obtaining it is less than the expected benefits it is expected to provide.

24 D

Internal information is information from an internal source. Information from the Institute of Directors, the tax authorities (e.g. HM Revenue and Customs in the UK) and a government department (national minimum wage) are all examples of external information – i.e. information from an external source.

25 A

The cost accounts will always include items of expenditure to be included in manufacturing costs (Answers B, C and D). The cost accounts, unlike the financial accounts, might exclude expenditure relating to financial costs (e.g. bank interest).

26 B

Definition B is the most complete and so the correct answer. Definitions A, C and D all describe aspects of the use or purpose of an office, but are not complete definitions.

27 A

Answer B is irrelevant to the question and answer D is incorrect: office manuals do facilitate the induction and training of new staff. It could be argued that both answers A and C are disadvantages of office manuals. Answer A is definitely a disadvantage: a strict interpretation of the rules does lead to inflexibility. Answer C is not necessarily correct, because office manuals do not necessarily cause bureaucracy and bureaucracy does not necessarily demotivate staff.

ANSWERS TO MULTIPLE CHOICE QUESTIONS : SECTION 2

28   C

The physical despatch of goods to a customer is an operational task, which would normally be carried out by warehousing and delivery staff, or by an order despatch team.

29   B

Individual transactions are recorded/listed in the books of prime entry and only daily totals (or periodic totals) – and limited information – need to be posted to the general ledger accounts. Books of prime entry therefore avoid the need to record as much data in the ledger accounts as would otherwise be necessary.

SOURCE DOCUMENTS AND CODING

30   B

The buyer prepares a purchase order. The supplier delivers the goods to the stores department and provides a delivery note. The stores department prepares a goods received note. The accounts department receives the goods received note from the stores department and the invoice from the supplier.

31   A

The sales process may begin with an enquiry from a potential customer. The customer then places the order. When the order is delivered, the customer is sent an invoice. The customer is then required to pay the invoice within the credit period allowed.

32   C

A purchase originates with a requisition for goods, by either the stores department or a user department. The buying department negotiates purchase terms and issues a purchase order to send to the supplier. The supplier processes the order and delivers the goods. A delivery note is provided with the goods when delivered. The stores department then produces its own document to record the goods received (the goods received note), which includes additional details such as the code for the item of inventory. The supplier sends the invoice when the goods are delivered. Invoices received from suppliers are called purchase invoices.

When the invoice has been checked and confirmed as correct, a cheque requisition might be prepared, for a senior manager to sign, asking the relevant section of the accounts department to prepare a cheque and send it to the supplier.

33   D

The price should be checked against a copy of the purchase order, or possibly against an official price list from the supplier. The purchase order should show the price the buyer has negotiated, including any discount. The quantity ordered might not be the same as the quantity delivered, so the quantity in the invoice should be checked against the goods received note. The goods received note is preferable to the delivery note, because the delivery note might be signed quickly, before the stores department has had time to check for faulty items or to carry out a detailed count of the items delivered.

MA1 : MANAGEMENT INFORMATION

34 C

The code for an item inventory should be entered on the goods received note by the stores clerk. This can be used for inputting the code to the computer system. If there is a risk of error, you might choose to double-check the code on the goods received note against a list of inventory codes. (The delivery note and purchase invoice are prepared by the supplier, so are unlikely to include an inventory code number from your own organisation.)

35 B

The accounts department deals with matters related to recording financial transactions, keeping accounting records and making and receiving payments. Its staff are most unlikely to do work in the stores department, receiving incoming deliveries of goods.

36 B

100 for Whitby followed by 420 for power followed by 620 for production. Power costs are most likely to be a production overhead cost, rather than a purchasing, finance or sales overhead cost.

37 D

Statements A, B and C are all correct. When codes are used, more data validation checks (such as existence checks, range checks and check digit checks) are possible. As a result, data processing should be more accurate. Codes are shorter than a description of the items they represent, so using codes speeds up processing too. A hierarchical code is also useful for learning and accessing code items. Using codes does not take away the need to understand the work that is being done or the items that are being processed, so statement D is incorrect.

38 B

In descending order:

TRO1214

TRO1100

TOR1102

TOP1213

The sorting is by the alphabetic characters first, not the numbers.

39 D

A check digit check is a form of data validation check. This type of check is carried out by the computer program to test an item in a record for logical errors. A check digit can be included within a code, such that if there is any error keying in the code, for example entering 1243 instead of 1234, the check digit check will automatically identify the error and report it for investigation and checking. Check digit checks can be a very useful form of data validation check to prevent input errors for key identification code items.

ANSWERS TO MULTIPLE CHOICE QUESTIONS : SECTION 2

40 C

In 'descending' order, given the fact that codes start with letters rather than numbers, means in reverse alphabetical order (and then in descending numerical order when two codes begin with the same four letters). The four items in descending order are therefore:

ADDA0100
ADAM0001
ADAA0099
ABAB0999

41 B

The buying department places a purchase order with the supplier. The supplier delivers the goods, and provides a delivery note with the delivery. A person in the stores department then prepares a goods received note from the details of the delivery note, adding extra details such as the code number of the stores item delivered. The supplier will send an invoice when the goods have been delivered. When the invoice has been authorised for payment, it might be necessary to prepare a cheque requisition, which is a form asking for a cheque to be prepared to make a payment. Finally, the cheque is prepared and sent to the supplier.

42 D

A goods received note is usually prepared by a member of staff in the stores department that takes receipt of the goods.

43 A

44 A

Option B describes a purchase requisition note. Option C describes a delivery note. Option D describes a material requisition note.

COST CLASSIFICATION AND MEASUREMENT

45 C

Prime cost is defined as the total direct production cost of an item. This consists of direct material and direct labour cost, plus any direct expenses.

46 C

This is a simple definition of a semi-fixed (or semi-variable) cost.

47 D

Material costs vary with the volume of production.

48 B

An overhead cost is an indirect cost. This is a cost that cannot be traced directly to a unit of production or sale, or any other cost unit. Overheads include indirect materials costs, indirect labour costs and indirect expenses (for example, factory rental costs, machinery insurance costs, machinery depreciation and so on).

KAPLAN PUBLISHING

MA1 : MANAGEMENT INFORMATION

49 B

A direct cost is a cost that can be traced directly to a unit of production or sale, or another cost unit. 'Economically' means that the benefit from identifying and tracing the direct cost to the cost unit must be worth the cost and the effort. In practice, this means that low-cost items, particularly low-cost material items, might be treated as indirect costs because the benefit from the greater 'accuracy' from treating them as direct material costs is not worth the cost and the effort.

50 B

It would be appropriate to use the costs for a batch of cakes, since the cost for an individual cake might be too small. The cost per kilogram might not relate to the same number of cakes, and the cost per production run might relate to different quantities of output.

51 B

Supervisors' salaries are most likely to behave as stepped costs because, as activity levels increase, more workers will be needed and therefore the number of supervisors will increase also. Supervisors are usually paid a fixed salary and so the costs of employing them will go up in a 'step'.

52 B

A would be a line parallel with the base line showing units. B would be a line commencing at '0' and would show a linear pattern. C would be linear but would start some way up the y axis. D would show a stepped effect, fixed for a short range, with successive increases.

53 C

Revenue is most likely to be based on the quantity delivered and the distance travelled. In addition, costs are likely to relate to both distance travelled and weight of load. Cost per tonne mile gives a measure of both quantity and distance.

54 B

	$
Total overhead cost of 15,100 square metres	83,585
Fixed overheads	21,675
Variable overhead cost of 15,100 square metres	61,910

Variable overhead cost per square metre = $61,910/15,100 = $4.10 per square metre.

Estimated overhead costs for 16,200 square metres can be found as follows:

	$
Variable cost of 16,200 square metres (× $4.10)	66,420
Fixed overheads	21,675
Total overhead cost of 16,200 square metres	88,095

ANSWERS TO MULTIPLE CHOICE QUESTIONS : SECTION 2

55 C

	$
Total cost of 18,500 hours	251,750
Total cost of 17,000 hours	246,500
Variable cost of 1,500 hours	5,250
The variable overhead rate per hour is thus	$3.50
Total cost of 17,000 hours	246,500
Less variable cost 17,000 × 3.50	59,500
Fixed cost	187,000

56 B

Power costs and depreciation charges are overhead costs. Materials used in production are a direct material cost. Costs incurred obtaining special tools for a specific job are a direct expense of that job.

57 B

Items (a) and (b) are direct material costs. Item (e) is a selling overhead cost. Item (f) is a direct labour cost. Item (h) is likely to be treated as an administration overhead.

58 D

A, B and C all relate to overhead cost, not 'direct expense'.

59 C

Answer C is the best definition of a cost centre. Answer A is incorrect, because this defines a cost unit. A cost centre is used to measure costs, but not revenues and profit, so answer B is incorrect. Although budgets are often prepared for cost centres, answer D is not exact enough as a definition: it could apply just as much to profit centres and responsibility centres.

60 D

Investment centre performance should be measured by taking into account both the profit earned and the amount of capital invested in the centre. Residual income is profit less a notional charge for interest on capital employed. Either residual income or Return on Capital Employed is therefore an appropriate performance measure for an investment centre.

61 C

Machining, finishing and assembly are all departments involved directly in the production of manufactured items. Despatch is a part of sales and distribution activities, and so is a sales and distribution overhead cost.

62 D

Although costs can be measured for each train in service, each train journey and for each passenger carried, it is more useful for comparative purposes to measure the average cost of carrying passengers a given distance, i.e. a cost per passenger/mile. Trains are of different sizes and journeys are of different lengths, so comparisons on the basis of cost per train or cost per journey would not have much meaning. (In a similar way, road haulage companies measure the cost per tonne/mile delivered as a cost unit.)

63 A

Courses vary in length and student numbers vary between courses. A suitable measure of cost would be the cost for one student for each day of training. For example, if a course lasts five days and the average cost per student per day is $30, the cost for the course would be $150 per student. A price can be worked out for the course by adding a profit margin to the cost of $150.

64 B

If the decision under review is whether to specialise in particular services, the most relevant information is the profitability for each type of service. This happens in practice: some law firms tend to specialise, for example in media law, employment law, criminal law and so on. If the decision had been whether to focus on a particular type of client, the relevant information would have been the profitability of providing services to each client type.

Similarly, if the decision had been about whether to shut down one of the offices, the relevant information would have been the profitability of the office. The relevant management information varies according to the decision for which it is required.

65 C

You can work this out by taking some illustrative numbers. For example, suppose that a firm has fixed costs of $2,400 per period. If it produces one unit in the period, the fixed cost per unit would be $2,400. If it produced two units, the fixed cost per unit would be $1,200. If it produced three units, the fixed cost per unit would be $800. If it produced four units, the fixed cost per unit would be $600. If it produced five units, the fixed cost per unit would be $480. The fixed cost per unit is falling as output increases, but at a declining rate.

66 A

Strictly speaking, all these items should be direct materials costs in building a house. However, material items with a low unit cost, such as nails and screws, are treated as indirect materials costs. This is because the time and effort required to measure low-cost items as direct costs is not worth the benefits obtained from the management accounting information it would produce.

67 D

The brochure costs are a common cost (overhead cost) for all holidays to all destinations. Air charter flight costs are a common cost for customers going to different hotels at the same destination, and so are an overhead cost. The only costs directly attributable to specific hotels are the hotel accommodation charges.

ANSWERS TO MULTIPLE CHOICE QUESTIONS : SECTION 2

68 B

The full cost of a unit is its direct cost (prime cost) plus a share of overhead costs (variable and fixed overhead). Full production cost could also be defined as the variable production cost plus a share of fixed production overheads.

69 C

Total fixed costs stay the same as output changes but fixed costs per unit fall. As output increases the fixed costs is shared over more units, and therefore the fixed cost per unit falls.

Heating cost is a fixed cost because it does not vary with the number of units of production. It may vary for many other reasons. B is the definition of a stepped cost. A semi-variable cost has a fixed and variable element. Unit variable costs stay constant as output changes, total variable costs change with the level of output.

70 D

The cost does not change for 300 and 400 units, therefore it cannot be variable or semi-variable. It changes between 200 and 300 units, so it cannot be a totally fixed cost. It must be a stepped cost.

71 D

Items A, B and C can be allocated to the cost of a job or batch. Depreciation would not generally be allocated to a job or batch and is an indirect cost.

72 A

Variable cost per unit is constant. Chart 2 is total variable cost.

73 B

Assembly is a direct production operation and so the assembly department is a production cost centre, not a service cost centre. Accounting and personnel are administration service centres and so the costs of these centres are likely to be treated as administration overhead.

74 D

The company is 'reviewing the range of goods to be stocked' in its branches. Its best method of analysing profitability is therefore by product or product line. The other methods of analysing profitability might all be valid, but not for the particular purpose specified in the question.

75 C

Rent, rates and the production director's salary would all be classified as fixed costs.

KAPLAN PUBLISHING

76 A

The manager is responsible for encouraging residents to use the hotel's catering facilities. Reports B and D would not distinguish between hotel residents and outside users of the facilities, and so would be inappropriate. Only Report A analyses the usage of the catering facilities by the hotel residents.

77 C

Items A, B and D would normally be drawn on a graph as a line parallel to the x axis (where the x axis represents volume of production and the y axis represents cost). The fixed cost per unit falls as the volume of output rises, and not in a straight line.

78 C

Strictly speaking, all four items in the question are direct materials and so direct material costs. In practice, however, it is usual to treat large volume low-unit-cost items as indirect materials, and so as an indirect material cost. Examples of such items are staples, nails, small pins, screws, and so on.

79 D

A cost unit is a unit of output, for a hotel the output can be in the form of one night stay in a room (room/night), it could be a meal served in the restaurant or it could be a conference delegate in the conference room.

80 B

Quantity surveying, planning, design & sales are all departments within a house building company which would incur costs & bungalows, town houses & detached houses are units of the product they sell.

81 C

Inventory is valued at marginal production cost, which is the prime cost plus any variable production overhead.

COST ACCOUNTING

82 C

	Hours
750 units should take (at 20 units per hour)	37.5
Did take	32.0
Time saved	5.5

ANSWERS TO MULTIPLE CHOICE QUESTIONS : SECTION 2

83 D

Unless overtime is worked specifically at the request of a particular customer, the cost of any overtime premium is treated as a general production overhead cost. The only direct labour cost is the cost of the hours worked, valued at the basic rate of pay per hour. Here, this cost is $27,500 + $4,500 = $32,000.

84 A

	$
600 units at $0.40	240.0
50 units at $0.50	25.0
10 units at $0.75	7.5
For 660 units	272.5

85 B

Piecework is an incentive-based pay scheme, because employees are paid more for producing more, and so have an incentive to be more productive. A high day rate scheme, in which employees receive a high basic rate of pay, does not offer an incentive to be more productive.

86 B

Working conditions, pension provisions and welfare are all costs associated with *retaining* labour, not *replacing* labour.

87 D

Paid hours including idle time = 2,400 × 100/80 = 3,000

Budgeted labour cost = 3,000 hours × $10 = $30,000

88 A

Productive hours	3,300
Idle time (3,300 × 25/(100 – 25))	1,100
Total paid hours	4,400
Total labour cost	$36,300
Labour rate per hour	$8.25

89 B

Managers are not usually classified as direct labour.

90 C

Idle time is an overhead cost. Unless overtime is worked specifically at the request of a particular customer, the cost of any overtime premium is treated as a general production overhead cost. However, when overtime is worked specifically for a customer, the overtime premium is treated as a direct cost of the job.

	$
42 hours less 4 hours idle time = 38 hours	
38 hours at basic rate of pay ($3.60)	136.80
Overtime premium for 2 hours (× 50% of $3.60)	3.60
Total direct wages cost	140.40

91 A

Good output = 240 – 8 = 232 units.

	$
100 units at $0.40	40.00
100 units at $0.50	50.00
32 units at $0.60	19.20
For 232 good units	109.20

92 A

Supervisor's wages are usually classified as a step cost because a supervisor may be responsible for supervising up to a specific number of workers. However, if output increases such that additional direct labour is required, then an extra supervisor will be required. Rates do step up in cost but that is in relation to time not output i.e. the rates may increase year on year.

93 C

Information on contracted rates of pay should be provided to the accounts office by the Human Resources (personnel) department.

94 D

A: idle time is partially controllable. B: not all internal factors are controllable. C cannot be production staff's responsibility.

ANSWERS TO MULTIPLE CHOICE QUESTIONS : SECTION 2

95 C

	$
Monday 90 × $0.2	18
Tuesday 70 × $0.2	15 (minimum guaranteed)
Wednesday 75 × $0.2	15 (minimum guaranteed)
Thursday 60 × $0.2	15 (minimum guaranteed)
Friday 90 × $0.2	18
Total	81

A incorrectly calculated as $15/day guarantee. B incorrectly based entirely on piecework earnings. D incorrectly calculated as piecework earnings + day rate guarantee.

96 D

This is a basic definition of overhead allocation.

97 B

A method of dealing with overheads which involves spreading common costs over cost centres on the basis of benefit received is known as overhead apportionment.

98 C

A supervisor's time is more likely to be spent on supervising employees in proportion to the direct labour hours worked.

99 C

Insurance costs for machinery are probably best apportioned in relation to the value of the machinery. However, like motor car insurance, the cost of the insurance depends not just on value, but also on other factors such as usage (e.g. car mileage each year/machine hours operated). Greater usage creates a greater risk of breakdown.

100 C

Production overheads can be absorbed by any of the methods listed in the question, except for indirect labour hours as, by definition, they do not have a strong correlation with output. A rate per unit is only appropriate when all units produced are identical.

101 D

Grade B labour costs are an indirect labour cost. Grade A labour costs are direct costs for the basic pay, but overtime premium is treated as an overhead cost if the overtime hours are worked as general overtime. If overtime is worked for a specific purpose, such as a customer order, the cost of overtime premium paid to direct labour is treated as a direct cost. The direct labour cost for the week is therefore:

30 hours worked in overtime	$
Cost of basic pay, Grade A labour (30 × $10)	300
Cost of overtime premium for hours on specific order (10 × 50% of $10)	50
	350

MA1 : MANAGEMENT INFORMATION

102 B

Although the basic hourly wage of direct labour employees is treated as a direct cost, even when the work is done in overtime, the cost of any overtime premium is usually treated as a production overhead (= factory overhead) cost.

103 B

Employees in a stores department in a factory are indirect workers and their labour costs are treated as a production overhead cost. Direct labour are employees directly engaged in producing the output of the business (e.g. assembly workers and building workers in a construction company), or in the case of a service organisation, delivering its chargeable services to customers (e.g. an audit clerk).

104 D

Apportionment means sharing out. With cost apportionment, a cost is shared out between two or more cost centres on a fair basis. For example, the rental cost of a building might be shared between the departments that occupy the building in proportion to the space taken up by each of them (in other words, on the basis of square metres).

105 D

Indirect costs	$
Grade B labour	
Basic wages (6 × 43 hours × $6)	1,548
Overtime premium (6 × 3 hours × $3)	54
Grade A labour	
Overtime premium (10 × 5 hours × 50% × $8)	200
	———
	1,802
	———

106 C

The term 'gross wages' means the total amount earned by employees before deductions for income tax, employees' state benefit contributions (National Insurance in the UK) and any other deductions from pay (such as pension contributions by the employee). The employer has to pay an additional tax on wages, the employer's state benefit contributions. These are included within the costs of labour in the management accounts. However, they are not an element in gross wages.

107 B

The total labour cost to the business is the cost of the salaries (= gross earnings) plus the employer's state benefit contributions (National Insurance in the UK). $23,000 + $3,500 = $26,500. The income tax and employees' state benefit contributions are deductions from salaries, and so are included within the salaries total.

ANSWERS TO MULTIPLE CHOICE QUESTIONS : SECTION 2

108 A

Good units produced = 380 – 35 = 345 units.

	$
First 200 units (× $0.60)	120
Next 100 units (× $0.80)	80
Next 45 units (× $1.00)	45
Gross earnings	245

109 D

Heating and lighting costs are probably related more to the area taken up by each department, rather than the number of employees or machines.

110 A

Management time spent dealing with each department is probably related to either the number of employees in each department or the hours worked in each department.

111 D

Free inventory is normally defined as the quantity currently in inventory plus the quantities due to be received (e.g. quantities on order) minus the quantities that have been requisitioned. 400 – 320 + 350 = 430.

112 D

		Direct costs $	Overheads $
Direct operatives: basic pay	(20 × 44 × $5)	4,400	–
Direct operatives: overtime premium	(20 × 6 × 50% of $5)	–	300
Indirect staff: basic pay	(10 × 44 × $5)	–	2,200
Indirect staff: overtime premium	(10 × 6 × 50% of $5)	–	150
		4,400	2,650

113 D

A fully absorbed cost consists of direct costs (usually variable costs) plus fixed and variable overheads.

114 A

The costs of payroll to the employer are the gross wages and salaries plus the employer's state benefit contribution (National Insurance in the UK). Income tax and employees' state benefit contributions are deductions out of gross wages and salaries, and so are a part of that cost.

KAPLAN PUBLISHING

MA1 : MANAGEMENT INFORMATION

115 A

Total production	210
Rejected items	17
Good output	193

	$
Pay for the first 100 units (× $0.20)	20.00
Pay for the next 93 units (× $0.30)	27.90
Employee's total earnings	47.90

116 B

The charging of an overhead expense item in full to a specific cost centre is called allocation. Apportionment means sharing a cost between two or more cost centres on a fair basis, and absorption is the charging of overhead costs to items of production (cost units) on a fair basis.

117 D

Insurance premiums for machinery are generally related to the value of the items insured, rather than to the number of items, their size or their rate of usage. Since the cost is most closely linked to asset values, apportionment on the basis of value is the most appropriate.

118 B

275 + 650 – 300 = 625 units

119 B

The basic pay of direct workers is a direct cost.

30 × 42 × $8 = $10,080

Indirect labour cost and the overtime premium are indirect costs.

120 D

Good units = 512 – 17 – 495

200 units at 15c + 295 units at 20c = $89

121 C

325 units took	180 hours
Standard time (325 × 36 / 60)	195 hours
So	15 hours were saved

Bonus = ½ × 15 × $8 = $60

ANSWERS TO MULTIPLE CHOICE QUESTIONS : SECTION 2

122 D

		$
Basic rate	72 hours × $10	720
Bonus	(108 − 72) × $\frac{36}{108}$ × $10	120
Total payment for job		840

123 C

	Job 812 $
Direct materials	60
Direct labour	40
Direct expenses	20
Prime cost	120
Production overheads ($40 ÷ 8) × $16	80
Non-production overheads (0.6 × $120)	72
Total cost – Job 812	272

124 D

Statement A is correct. Job costs are identified with a particular job, whereas process costs (of units produced and work in process) are averages, based on equivalent units of production.

Statement B is also correct. The direct cost of a job to date, excluding any direct expenses, can be ascertained from materials requisition notes and job tickets or time sheets.

Statement C is correct, because without data about units completed and units still in process, losses and equivalent units of production cannot be calculated.

Statement D is incorrect, because the cost of normal loss will usually be incorporated into job costs as well as into process costs. In process costing this is commonly done by giving normal loss no cost, leaving costs to be shared between output, closing inventory and abnormal loss/gain. In job costing it can be done by adjusting direct materials costs to allow for normal wastage, and direct labour costs for normal reworking of items or normal spoilage.

125 D

	Job 1	Job 2	Total
	$	$	$
Opening WIP	8,500	0	8,500
Material in period	17,150	29,025	46,175
Labour for period	12,500	23,000	35,500
Overheads (see working)	43,750	80,500	124,250
	81,900	132,525	214,425

Working

Total labour cost for period = $(12,500 + 23,000 + 4,500) = $40,000

Overhead absorption rate = $140,000/$40,000 = 3.5 times the direct labour cost.

126 C

	Job 3
	$
Opening WIP	46,000
Labour cost for period	4,500
Overheads (350% × $4,500)	15,750
Total production costs	66,250
Profit (50%)	33,125
Selling price of 2,400 boards	99,375

Selling price of one board = $99,375/2,400 = $41.41

127 B

Cost per unit = net process costs/expected output

= (9,000 + 13,040)/(2,000 − 100)

= $22,040/1,900 = $11.60.

128 B

The total value of WIP will increase. The number of equivalent units will increase which will cause the cost per unit to decrease.

129 C

Note: do not include non-production overheads

Total production cost of batch = 3,000 + (120 × 5) + (120 × 12) = $5,040

Cost per shirt = 5,040 ÷ 200 = $25.20.

ANSWERS TO MULTIPLE CHOICE QUESTIONS : SECTION 2

130 C

Note: do include non-production overheads

Total cost of batch = 7,000 + 3,600 + (80 × 10) + (40 × 5) + (80 × 15) = $12,800

Cost per meal = 12,800 ÷ 10,000 = $1.28.

131 D

Process cost = (1,000 × 5) + 11,000 = $16,000

Expected good output = actual output = 800 litres

Cost per litre = 16,000 / 800 = $20

132 D

| Started | => | Finished | + | CWIP |
| 1,300 | => | 800 (to balance) | + | 500 |

Finished units are 100% complete for both material and conversion.

Equivalent units			Costs	
Completed in period EU	CWIP EU	Total EU	Total costs ($)	Costs per EU ($)
800	400 (80% × 500)	1,200	7,200	6.00
800	250 (50% × 500)	1,050	4,200	4.00
			11,400	10.00

133 D

Senior	86 hours at $20	$1,720
Junior	220 hours at $15	$3,300
Overheads	306 hours at $12.50	$3,825
Total cost		$8,845
Mark-up	(40%)	$3,538
Selling price		$12,383

134 B

MA1 : MANAGEMENT INFORMATION

135 B

Using FIFO, inventory is issued at the earliest price.

The issue on the 19 January would be made up of 500 costing		$1,250
	1,000 costing	$2,750
	600 × $2.80	$1,680
The issue on the 31 January would be made up of 1,000 × $2.80		$2,800
	800 × 2.90	$2,320
Total issue value		$10,800

136 C

Using LIFO, the 1,900 units of closing inventory is valued as the opening inventory of 500 units ($1,250) plus the 1,000 units received on 4 January ($2,750) plus 400 of the units received on 11 January, which have a value of $4,480 × 400/1,600 = $1,120.

	$
500 units of opening inventory	1,250
1,000 units received on 4 January	2,750
400 units received on 11 January	1,120
Total value of closing inventory	5,120

137 D

With average cost (AVCO), a new average cost only needs to be calculated before there is an issue from stores.

	Units	Total cost $	Average cost $
Opening inventory	500	1,250	
Receipts on 4 January	1,000	2,750	
Receipts on 11 January	1,600	4,480	
Receipts on 18 January	1,200	3,480	
	4,300	11,960	$2.78
Issues on 19 January	(2,100)	(5,838)	$2.78
	2,200	6,122	
Receipts on 25 January	1,500	4,350	
	3,700	10,472	**$2.83**
Issues on 31 January	(1,800)	(5,094)	**$2.83**
	1,900	5,378	

138 A

	Units	Unit cost $	Total $
Opening inventory	100	3.00	300
3 March receipt	200	3.50	700
	300		1,000
8 March issue	(250)	200 at 3.50	(700)
		50 at 3.00	(150)
	50	3.00	150
15 March receipt	300	3.20	960
17 March receipt	200	3.30	660
	550		1,770
21 March issue	(500)	200 at 3.30	(660)
		300 at 3.20	(960)
	50	3.00	150
23 March receipt	450	3.10	1,395
	500		1,545
27 March issue	(350)	3.10	(1,085)
Closing balance	150		460

The closing inventory balance represents 50 units at $3 and 100 units at $3.10.

139 B

	Units	Unit cost $	Total $
Opening inventory	100	3.00	300
3 March receipt	200	3.50	700
	300	3.333	1,000
8 March issue	(250)	3.333	(833)
	50	3.333	167
15 March receipt	300	3.20	960
17 March receipt	200	3.30	660
	550	3.249	1,787
21 March issue	(500)	3.249	(1,625)
	50	3.249	162
23 March receipt	450	3.10	1,395
	500	3.114	1,557
27 March issue	(350)	3.114	(1,090)
Closing balance	150	3.114	467

Issues = $833 + $1,625 + $1,090 = $3,548

MA1 : MANAGEMENT INFORMATION

140 B

With FIFO, the issues on 9 September are valued as follows:

	$
60 units of the opening inventory brought forward (at $5)	300
10 units received on 4 June (at $5.50)	55
Total value	355

141 C

With LIFO, the issues on 9 September are valued as follows:

	$
50 units received on 6 June (at $6)	300
20 units received on 4 June (at $5.50)	110
Total value	410

142 D

A and C are relevant only to physical inventory movement.

B is a description of the LIFO method.

143 A

B and D are incorrect as material costs which are lower, reduce cost.

C is incorrect as lower costs lead to higher profit.

144 B

	Kg
Required for production (6,000 × 2.5)	15,000
Required closing inventory (1,800 × 2/3)	1,200
	16,200
Expected opening inventory	1,800
Therefore budgeted purchase quantities	14,400

ANSWERS TO MULTIPLE CHOICE QUESTIONS : SECTION 2

145 D

	Units of T	Units of X
Sales budget	5,000	
Increase in finished goods inventory	200	
Production budget	5,200	
Required for production (5,200 × 3)		15,600
Increase in closing inventory		400
Therefore budgeted purchase quantities		16,000

146 C

Production budget

Sales	8,000
+ closing inventory	1,500
– opening inventory	2,000
	7,500

Usage budget = 7,500 units × 1.2 kg per unit = 9,000 kgs

Purchases budget:

usage	9,000
+ closing inventory	2,400
– opening inventory	1,500
	9,900 kgs

THE SPREADSHEET SYSTEM

147 C

By definition.

148 B

A spreadsheet program can convert numerical data into the form of a graph, pie chart or bar chart, as required, but it cannot produce a narrative description.

149 C

A database contains records and files and is most suitable for storing large volumes of data

150 B

All are said to be advantages of spreadsheet software with the exception of (i) security.

A computer-based approach exposes the firm to threats from viruses, hackers and general system failure.

MA1 : MANAGEMENT INFORMATION

151 D

Budgeted production for a period = budgeted sales for the period + closing inventory of finished goods for the period –opening inventory of finished goods for the period.

Here

F3 + 10% of F4 – 10% of F3 = budgeted production for March

152 B

Using graphics is usually done using the chart wizard not the format cells option.

153 A

B would be done best via a face to face discussion and a spreadsheet would not feature strongly.

C would be best done using a word processing package.

D would be best done using a database.

154 C

The correct syntax has an = sign and a colon.

155 D

Depending on which number formatting category you select, you will be able to adjust the following characteristics:

	Decimal Places	Negative number format	1000 Separator	Currency symbol
Number	Yes	Yes	Yes	–
Currency	Yes	Yes	Auto	Yes
Accounting	Yes	–	Auto	Yes
Percentage	Yes	–	–	–

156 C

Depending on which number formatting category you select, you will be able to adjust the following characteristics:

	Decimal Places	Negative number format	1000 Separator	Currency symbol
Number	Yes	Yes	Yes	–
Currency	Yes	Yes	Auto	Yes
Accounting	Yes	–	Auto	Yes
Percentage	Yes	–	–	–

ANSWERS TO MULTIPLE CHOICE QUESTIONS : SECTION 2

157 C

In this respect spreadsheets follow the usual rules for the use of brackets

158 B

Pie charts will be least effective to show trends but both of the others will work, although you could argue that the line chart is best.

159 B

Error	Description
#DIV/0!	This occurs where we have tried to divide by zero or a blank cell.
#NAME?	This occurs when we use a name that Excel doesn't recognise. This is common in incorrectly spelled function names
#NUM!	This occurs when you place an invalid argument in a function
#REF!	This occurs when a formula uses an invalid cell reference
#VALUE!	This occurs when we attempt to use an incorrect data type

160 C

Error	Description
#DIV/0!	This occurs where we have tried to divide by zero or a blank cell.
#NAME?	This occurs when we use a name that Excel doesn't recognise. This is common in incorrectly spelled function names
#NUM!	This occurs when you place an invalid argument in a function
#REF!	This occurs when a formula uses an invalid cell reference
#VALUE!	This occurs when we attempt to use an incorrect data type

161 A

An entire page is a worksheet (a workbook may have many worksheets) and columns are identified by letters not numbers.

162 D

(1) is false – while formula can be copied from one cell to another, the formula in a particular cell will only give the value for that cell. Other cells may then use this answer in their own formulae.

(2) is false – Control+end takes you to the cell furthest into the worksheet that has been active [even if the content has been removed]

MA1 : MANAGEMENT INFORMATION

163 A

Formatting is concerned with appearance and seeks to make the spreadsheet look more interesting and make it reflect the underlying data better. Thus a number format may be better than plain text (hence (4) is wrong). Formatting is not concerned with ordering, so statement (2) is incorrect.

164 B

Wrap text increases the height of a row so that all text is visible.

165 C

The default print options are portrait, A4 without gridlines.

166 D

Line graphs are very useful to demonstrate trends.

167 D

Accounting information is usually confidential and should not be given to anyone without the proper authority.

168 B

The Ctrl key + P will bring up the Print function, which will then print if you click on OK.

169 B

The number will appear as you typed it.

170 D

The number will appear with a percentage sign after it. Most Excel spreadsheets will work to two decimal places by default.

171 A

Rounding 10.567 will give 11.

172 B

The symbol $ makes a cell address absolute.

173 A

Total commission = total saes × 5% = (home sales + overseas sales) × 5%

ANSWERS TO MULTIPLE CHOICE QUESTIONS : SECTION 2

174 D

The standard 40 hour week needs to be 'held' to compare with the employees actual hours in cells C10 to C14. Using the $ sign next to B and 2 will do this.

175 A

To SORT the price column C, you would need to select the data range A2:C5, right click, data, sort, choose to sort column C.

176 B

A component bar chart shows the total sales in any one year. The individual components of each bar should show the sales mix for the three different products.

177 C

Given we are looking at a single period, a pie chart would be the most useful for showing the overall split.

178 D

Management accounting reports should be understandable by non-financial managers. It is totally misguided to think that all managers should be financially literate, and it is important to make sure that reports to non-financial managers are clear and well presented, and that difficult or unusual issues are explained carefully.

179 C

The first two explanations are not related to three dimensional spreadsheets. The final description is not three dimensional as the workbooks are not linked together. Option C is the correct definition.

180 D

181 A

See Chapter 19, section 7.3 of the text for a full explanation of the round function.

182 B

Spreadsheets are commonly used for internal, management accounting information such as variance reports, budgets and forecasts. The annual accounts are more likely to use word processing or publishing software (or even specialist accounting software) as they will involve more words and fewer calculations.

183 A

This is the order in which the symbols will be interpreted when entered into a spreadsheet formula.

MA1 : MANAGEMENT INFORMATION

184 A

All selected columns will be hidden. So if three columns are selected, three will be hidden.

185 B

It would not be possible to select the hidden row as it is hidden. A user must select the rows above and below the hidden row or rows.

186 B

The password to open option would not allow the user to even view the spreadsheet without entering a password. The 'read only recommended' option simply makes a recommendation to the user not to make changes, but the user can choose to make changes if they wish. The password to modify option will prompt the user to enter a password before making changes and is the correct answer.

187 B

188 D

There must be two parts to the custom format – one for positive numbers and one for negative numbers. So this rules out option A. The two parts must be separated by a semi-colon – this rules out option B. To show negative numbers with brackets the second part of the format must be surrounded by brackets. Therefore, option D is the correct answer.

189 D

There must be three parts to the custom format when we want to show zeros as blanks – one for positive numbers, one for negative numbers and one for zeros. So this rules out options A and C. To show zeros as blanks the third part must be blank – this rules out option B. Option D is the correct answer.

190 C

The time format must be split by a colon. The other answers will appear as text rather than as a time format (which can then be used in formulae etc.).

191 B

The spreadsheet won't recognise the text 'Four' as a number and will remind the user to input a number rather than text.

192 D

Option D alludes to a disadvantage of bar charts. If the bar chart is split into components it is more difficult to see the overall total.

ANSWERS TO MULTIPLE CHOICE QUESTIONS : SECTION 2

193 C

Line graphs will identify trends as it will be easy to see upward or downward patterns as well as peaks and troughs for seasonality.

194 D

The other graphs/charts rely on some correlation between the variables. A scatter graph is more likely to illustrate a random pattern or non-relationship.

195 D

196 B

Legend refers to the key and using the legend option allows a user to determine where the key gets displayed on a chart (for example, a user can choose to have it at the side or underneath the chart).

197 B

198 D

199 A

200 A

201 A

202 B

Section 3

MOCK EXAM QUESTIONS

ALL 50 QUESTIONS ARE COMPULSORY AND MUST BE ATTEMPTED

1 The following statements relate to financial accounting or to cost and management accounting:

   (i) Financial accounts are historical records.

   (ii) Cost accounting is part of financial accounting and establishes costs incurred by an organisation.

   (iii) Management accounting is used to aid planning, control and decision making.

   Which of the statements are correct?

   A   (i) and (ii) only

   B   (i) and (iii) only

   C   (ii) and (iii) only

   D   (i), (ii) and (iii)

2 **Which of the following is *not* necessarily a quality of good management information?**

   A   Timeliness

   B   Relevance

   C   Understandability

   D   Prudence

3 **Which of the following statements concerning data and information is true?**

   A   Information and data are two words used to describe the same thing.

   B   Information consists of raw facts and figures that have yet to be processed.

   C   Data consists of information that has been processed in a predefined way.

   D   Information consists of data that has been processed in a predefined way.

4 Payments to suppliers are entered into an integrated computerised accounting system.

Which of the following does *not* happen when these payments are entered into the computerised system?

- A   The supplier's individual account is updated in the purchase ledger/payables ledger.
- B   The payables control account in the nominal ledger (main ledger) is debited.
- C   The bank account in the nominal ledger is credited.
- D   The receivables control account in the nominal ledger is credited.

5 **Integrated accounts application packages have a number of advantages. Which of the following is *not* one of them?**

- A   User-friendly, as the functions will be similar in each module
- B   Tailored to suit the requirements of the business
- C   Compatibility between the modules
- D   Efficiency, as there is no need to quit one application to access another

6 **In a large organisation, which of the following individuals is most likely to authorise the payment of a purchase invoice for goods bought from a supplier?**

A manager with appropriate authority in the:

- A   accounts department
- B   buying department
- C   department that requisitioned the goods
- D   stores department

7 What is the main purpose of books of prime entry?

- A   Assist the preparation of financial statements
- B   Assist the monthly bank reconciliation
- C   Provide a check on the double-entry bookkeeping
- D   Prevent unnecessary detail in the ledgers

8 Noel is considering introducing a number of control systems into his business. However, he is uncertain about what this would accomplish. Which of the following is NOT a purpose of organisational control systems?

- A   Safeguarding of company assets
- B   Prevention of errors
- C   Increased profitability
- D   Increased efficiency

9 In an interlocking accounting system what would be the correct double entry for the issue of direct materials from a warehouse?

- A   Dr Raw material inventory   Cr Work in progress
- B   Dr Raw material inventory   Cr Production overhead
- C   Dr Work in progress   Cr Raw material inventory
- D   Dr Production overhead   Cr Raw material inventory

10 Management information is used at different levels of the organisation

(i)   Information used by strategic management tends to be summarised.

(ii) Information used by strategic management tends to be forward looking.

(iii) information used by operational management tends to contain estimates.

(iv) information used by operational management tends to be required frequently.

Which of the above statements are true?

- A   (i), (ii) and (iv) only
- B   (i), (iii) and (iv) only
- C   (ii) and (iii) only
- D   (iii) and (iv) only

11 What document may be used to authorise the issue of items from the stores department to a user department?

- A   Purchase order
- B   Delivery note
- C   Requisition note
- D   Goods received note

12 The current inventory position for inventory item 35528 is as follows:

	Units
Held in inventory	14,500
On order from supplier	36,300
Requisitioned	16,700

What is the free inventory for this item?

- A   0
- B   5,100 units
- C   34,100 units
- D   38,500 units

13 The following documents are used within a cost accounting system:

(i) invoice from supplier

(ii) purchase order

(iii) purchase requisition

(iv) stores requisition

Which TWO of the documents are matched with the goods received note in the buying process?

A (i) and (ii)

B (i) and (iv)

C (ii) and (iii)

D (iii) and (iv)

14 Which of the following items of cost cannot be treated as a sales and distribution overhead expense within a manufacturing business?

A Cost of after-sales service to customers

B Telephone charges

C Cost of building insurance

D Warehouse rental for storage of raw materials

15 An engineering business has a department with a work force of eight engineers and one supervisor. The department carries out small engineering jobs for business customers.

Which of the following costs would be treated as a direct expense of a particular job for a customer?

A Supervision costs

B Cost of delivery of equipment to the customer

C Depreciation of engineering equipment

D Cost of engineer's time on the job

16 Which of the following is an example of external information?

A Idle time reports

B Sales price lists

C Health and safety regulations

D Accident at work reports

17 Which ONE of the following would be classified as direct labour?

A Personnel manager in a company servicing cars

B Cleaner in a cleaning company

C General manager in a DIY shop

D Maintenance manager in a company producing cameras

18 Which of the following may be used to support claims for overtime payments for salaried staff?

- A Employee record cards
- B Job cards
- C Payslips
- D Timesheets

19 In accounting systems, data is usually organised using codes.

Which one of the following statements about codes is *incorrect*?

- A Using codes helps to improve the speed and accuracy of data processing
- B Using codes allows more data validation checks to be carried out
- C A hierarchical code structure makes it easier to find items on a code list, since similar items are grouped
- D Codes in accounting reduce the need for accountants to understand the principles of accounting

20 Gregs Ltd operates from four main sites. In analysing its costs (overheads) it uses a nine digit coding system. A sample from the coding manual shows:

Site		Expenditure type		Function	
Wokingham	100	Rent	410	Purchasing	600
Windsor	200	Power	420	Finance	610
Winchester	300	Heat and light	430	Production	620
Warwick	400	Travel costs	440	Sales	630

The order of coding is: site/expense/function

An invoice for the Windsor site for travel costs for sales teams would be coded as:

- A 200/410/600
- B 200/420/610
- C 200/430/620
- D 200/440/630

MA1 : MANAGEMENT INFORMATION

21 The performance of an investment centre is measured by residual income. In a particular period, the investment centre had fixed assets of $200,000 and net current assets of $40,000. Its annual profits were as follows:

	$	$
Sales price		217,000
Direct costs of the division	175,000	
Apportioned head office costs	15,000	
Total divisional costs		190,000
Profit		27,000

The notional interest on capital is 8%.

What was the residual income for the centre for the year?

A $7,800

B $11,000

C $22,800

D $26,000

22 **Which of the following measures of performance is unsuitable for a profit centre?**

A Sales income per employee

B Profit as a percentage of sales revenue

C Return on capital employed

D Cost per machine hour operated

23 **Which of the following statements is incorrect?**

A There may be several investment centres within a single organisation

B There may be several cost centres within an investment centre

C There may be several cost centres within a profit centre

D There may be several profit centres within a cost centre

24 **In a system of absorption costing, why are the absorption rates for fixed overheads usually determined in advance, as part of the budget, instead of retrospectively at the end of the budget period?**

A It is simpler to decide overhead rates in advance than retrospectively.

B It is not possible to calculate actual overhead costs retrospectively.

C So that fixed overheads can be charged to output before the end of the accounting period.

D Predetermined overheads are more accurate than overhead costs calculated retrospectively.

25 The annual costs of supervision in a department are estimated to be $40,000 if hours worked in the department are less than 32,000 each year, $65,000 if hours worked are between 32,000 and 50,000 and $80,000 if hours worked are over 50,000 in the year. These costs are an example of:

A   a semi-fixed cost

B   a fixed cost

C   a stepped cost

D   a variable cost

26 You are presented with the following information about sales and costs for a business that makes and sells a range of products:

	$
Sales revenue	320,000
Direct labour	100,000
Direct material	75,000
Production overhead	78,000
Other overhead costs	50,000

The business uses absorption costing. There were no opening or closing inventories of the product.

What profit would be reported for the period, using absorption costing?

A $15,000

B $17,000

C $20,000

D $23,000

27 Which of the following statements IS true when applied to fixed costs:

A   Overhead costs are always fixed costs

B   As production levels increase, fixed cost per unit decreases

C   Fixed costs are always irrelevant in a decision making situation

D   as the level of activity changes, fixed costs will also change

28 Which of the following cost classifications is most useful for forecasting?

A   Direct v indirect

B   Production v non-production

C   Fixed v variable

D   Controllable v non-controllable

29 Hannah works as a trainee accountant for a large accountancy firm. She is salaried and each month completes a time sheet indicating how much time she has spent working on which clients. In March Hannah's time was fully utilized on client work but she didn't do any overtime.

From her firm's perspective, how should Hannah's salary costs for March be classified?

A   Fixed   Direct
B   Fixed   Indirect
C   Variable   Direct
D   Variable   Indirect

30 A company achieves bulk buying discounts on quantities of raw material above a certain level. These discounts are only available for the units above the specified level and not on all the units purchased.

Which of the following graphs of total purchase cost against units best illustrates the above situation?

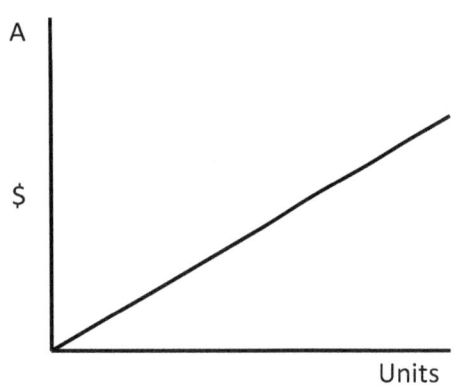
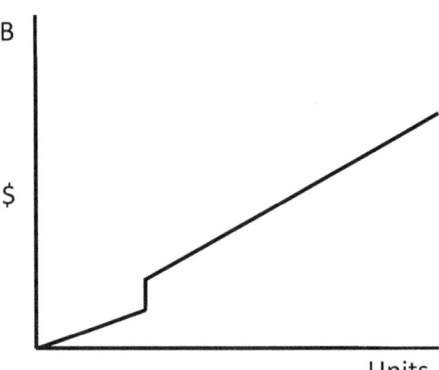
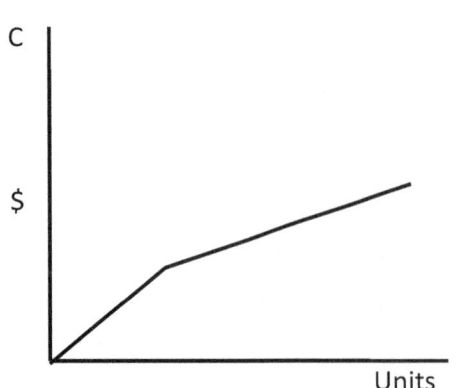
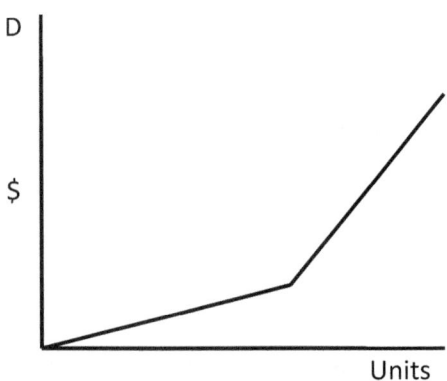

MOCK EXAM QUESTIONS : SECTION 3

31 A direct labour employee receives a wage of $8 per hour for a 38-hour week, with time + 25% for overtime. During a particular week, the employee worked for 42 hours. Due to an equipment breakdown and the late delivery of urgent materials from a supplier, the employee had to record six hours of idle time for the week.

What amount will be charged as a direct labour cost for the employee's work in the week?

A $288
B $296
C $304
D $336

32 A manufactured product requires two units of raw materials, each costing $5. The following budget decisions have been made for the next budget period.

	Product units
Sales volume	9,000
	Materials units
Opening inventory of raw materials	3,500
Closing inventory of raw materials	2,800

What is the raw materials purchase requirement for the period?

A $76,500
B $83,500
C $86,500
D $93,500

33 The following information is available for a small business with three departments, A, B and C that all operate in the same building.

Department	A	B	C
Floor area (square metres)	1,500	2,000	1,500
Number of employees	10	6	4
Assets	$40,000	$40,000	$80,000
Labour hours per month	1,200	1,000	800

Employees are provided with free lunchtime meals, and the cost of this small 'canteen' service is $1,800 per month.

If the businesses uses an absorption costing system, what would be the most appropriate charge to department A each month for the cost of the canteen service?

A $540
B $900
C $450
D $720

MA1 : MANAGEMENT INFORMATION

34 The following data relates to a company's payroll for the month just ended:

	$
Paid to employees	67,000
Employees' National Insurance contributions	21,000
Employer's National Insurance contributions	13,200
Income tax	36,300
Employer's contribution to employees' pension fund	15,000

What is the total labour cost for the month?

A $152,500

B $139,300

C $137,500

D $124,300

35 A product uses 6 kilograms of raw material and takes two direct labour hours to make. Raw materials cost $2.50 per kilogram and direct labour is paid $4 per hour. Variable production overheads are 25% of labour costs. The budgeted fixed production costs for the year were $120,000 and budgeted direct labour hours were 20,000 hours. Fixed overheads are recovered on a direct labour hour basis.

The full production cost per unit of product is:

A $25

B $31

C $35

D $37

36 Which of the following would operate a job costing system?

A Shipbuilder

B Oil refinery

C Steel producer

D Kitchen fitter

37 Completed output from a manufacturing process in a period totalled 5,640 units. There was no work-in-progress at the beginning of the period but 780 units, 60% complete, remained in the process at the end of the period.

What are the equivalent units of the closing work-in-progress?

A 312

B 468

C 780

D 6,108

38 A manufacturing process had no work-in-progress at the beginning of a period. 20,000 units of raw material, costing $8.20 per unit, were input to the process in the period. 18,600 completed units were transferred out. Conversion costs were $7.65 per completed unit and $6.12 per incomplete unit.

What was the value of the closing work-in-progress?

A $8,568

B $20,048

C $22,190

D $30,788

39 A company values stocks using the weighted average value after each purchase. The following materials receipts and issues were made last month:

Date	Receipts			Issues
	Units	$/unit	Valuation	Units
Brought forward	100	$5.00	$500	
4th	150	$5.50	$825	
16th				100
20th	100	$6.00	$600	
21st				75

What is the value of the closing stock using this weighted average method?

A $1,012.50

B $976.50

C $962.50

D $925.00

40 A firm has a high level of stock turnover and uses the FIFO (first in first out) issue pricing system. In a period of rising purchase prices, the closing stock valuation is:

A   close to current purchase prices

B   based on the prices of the first items received

C   much lower than current purchase prices

D   the average of all goods purchased in the period

41 Which of the following symbols are used in spreadsheet software?

(i)   /

(ii)   *

(iii)   ^

(iv)   ×

A   (ii) and (iii)

B   (i), (ii) and (iii)

C   (ii), (iii) and (iv)

D   All of them

MA1 : MANAGEMENT INFORMATION

42 Which of the following are disadvantages of spreadsheets?

(i) Inability to efficiently identify data errors

(ii) Finite number of records

(iii) Most data managers are familiar with them

(iv) Lack of detailed sorting and querying abilities

A (i) and (iv)

B (i), (iii) and (iv)

C (i), (ii) and (iv)

D All of them

43 Which of the following are advantages of spreadsheet software over manual approaches?

(i) Security

(ii) Speed

(iii) Accuracy

(iv) Legibility

A All of them

B (ii), (iii) and (iv)

C (ii) and (iv)

D (i) and (iv)

44 For which of the following tasks would a computer spreadsheet be most useful?

A Cost coding structure

B Product listing

C Staff appraisal

D Variance analysis

45 A business wants to organise its operational data into a computer system for the entire organisation that will allow multiple-user access to files. Which of the following types of general-purpose application package would be most suitable for this purpose?

A Word processing

B Spreadsheet

C Integrated accounts

D Database

46 The following spreadsheet shows an extract from a company's sales figures.

	A	B	C	D	E
1	Sales		2011	2012	2013
2	Region				
3	N		10,000	12,000	11,500
4	S		7,000	6,200	8,200
5	E		3,000	10,000	12,000
6	W		1,500	5,750	5,600

The management accountant wishes to produce a chart to demonstrate the trends over time between the different regions and is considering the following charts:

(i) Stacked (compound) bar chart

(ii) Line charts

(iii) Pie charts

Which of the charts would be suitable?

A (i) only

B (i) and (ii)

C (ii) only

D (i), (ii) and (iii)

47 Examine the following spreadsheet extract:

	A	B	C	D
1	Sales Month	Product X	Product Y	Total
2	Jan	10,000	50,000	60,000
3	Feb	14,000	6,000	20,000
4	Mar	12,000	TBC	

The formula in cell D2 is: =B2+C2. If this formula was copied to cell D4, which error message would appear?

A #DIV/0!

B #VALUE!

C #REF!

D #NAME?

48 **To unhide a hidden row, a user must first select**

A The entire worksheet

B The entire workbook

C The row that is hidden

D The rows above and below the hidden row

MA1 : MANAGEMENT INFORMATION

49 Examine the following spreadsheet extract for a budget calculation:

	A	B	C
1	**Budget for May**		**$000**
2	Sales		120
3	Cost of sales		(50)
4	Gross profit		70
5	Selling and distribution costs		(30)
6	Operating profit		40

Which formula in cell C6 will give the correct figure for the operating profit?

A =SUM(C2:C5)

B =C4-C5

C =C2-C3-C5

D =SUM(C4:C5)

50 Which of the following are reasons for formatting data in a spreadsheet?

(1) To make text (i.e. labels) more visually interesting

(2) To get data into the correct order for analysis

(3) To make numbers more descriptive of what they represent

(4) To make the data appear as plain text

A (1) and (3) only

B (2) and (3) only

C (2) and (4) only

D (1), (2) and (3)

Section 4

ANSWERS TO MOCK EXAM QUESTIONS

1 B

Cost accounting is not part of financial accounting.

2 D

Prudence is a desirable quality in financial accounting information, for reporting to shareholders. However, it is not necessarily a quality in management information. Management might wish to be prudent when making their judgements and decisions, but they do not need prudence in the information they receive.

3 D

By definition

4 D

This question is not testing your knowledge of debits and credits. It is checking that you understand the basic workings of an accounts system. When a payment is made to a supplier, a single entry into the integrated computer system will update the supplier's individual account in the payables/creditors/purchase ledger, and it will update the bank account and the payables control account in the nominal ledger. The receivables control account is unaffected by payments to suppliers.

5 B

With an integrated accounts system, the system consists of several applications or modules, such as nominal ledger, sales ledger, purchase ledger, inventory control system, payroll, management accounting, and so on. Each module is compatible with the others, and functions are similar in each module. They are efficient, because a user does not have to quit one module to enter another (which would be necessary if the accounts system consisted of different non-integrated applications).

However, when an integrated system is purchased 'off-the-shelf' (i.e. when it is an 'applications package') the user must take it as it comes, and the system is not tailored exactly to the user's requirements.

6 B

The accounts department should be instructed to make the payment, but should not authorise the payment itself. The authorisation for a payment should come from the department that can check that the purchase invoice details agree with the purchase order details and the goods received note details. The purchase order will not be seen by the stores department, nor by the department requisitioning the goods.

KAPLAN PUBLISHING

MA1 : MANAGEMENT INFORMATION

7 D

The main purpose of books of prime entry is to allow the main double entry into the nominal ledger to comprise totals – for example posting the total sales for the month to the sales account rather than showing every individual invoice.

8 C

Control systems may indirectly improve profitability through increased efficiency, etc., but it is not one of their primary purposes.

9 C

The credit entry must recognise that the materials have been taken out of inventory, so answers A and B are incorrect. Given the materials are "direct", then the debit entry must be to WIP (C) rather than overheads (D).

10 A

(iii) is incorrect as operational level information is usually accurate.

11 C

A materials requisition note is a document requesting materials from stores. It should be signed by a person with authority to make the requisition.

12 C

	Units
Held in inventory	14,500
On order from supplier	36,300
	50,800
Requisitioned	16,700
Free inventory	34,100

13 A

An invoice is matched to a goods received note and a purchase order before payment is made.

14 D

Sales and distribution overhead costs should include telephone charges for telephones used by the sales and distribution department and the costs of after-sales service. The sales and distribution department should also receive an apportioned share of building insurance costs for the building it occupies.

In a manufacturing business, rental costs for the raw materials warehouse are a production overhead cost.

ANSWERS TO MOCK EXAM QUESTIONS : SECTION 4

15 B

A direct cost is a cost that is directly attributable. Here, the direct costs of the job are the costs that are directly attributable to that job. Supervision costs and depreciation of equipment are general overhead costs for the department, and so would be treated as overheads. The costs of delivery and wages costs are both direct costs, but the wages cost is a direct labour cost. The delivery charge would be a direct expense.

16 C

External information is information that comes from outside the organisation, and is not generated from within the organisation. It includes rules and regulations from external bodies, government statistics, tax rates, information from customers or suppliers, and so on. Price lists for the organisation's own products, idle time records and accident records are all internal information.

17 B

Cleaner in a cleaning company.

The cleaner's wages can be identified with a specific cost unit therefore this is a direct cost. The wages paid to the other three people cannot be identified with specific cost units. Therefore they would be indirect costs.

18 D

19 D

Statements A, B and C are all correct. When codes are used, more data validation checks (such as existence checks, range checks and check digit checks) are possible. As a result, data processing should be more accurate. Codes are shorter than a description of the items they represent, so using codes speeds up processing too. A hierarchical code is also useful for learning and accessing code items. Using codes does not take away the need to understand the work that is being done or the items that are being processed, so statement D is incorrect.

20 D

21 A

	$
Profit	27,000
Notional interest (8% × $240,000)	19,200
Residual income	7,800

KAPLAN PUBLISHING

MA1 : MANAGEMENT INFORMATION

22   C

Performance measures for a profit centre should include measures of profit, such as gross profit margin and net profit margin (profit to sales ratio). They might also include measures of performance relating to sales income (e.g. sales per employee) and performance relating to cost (e.g. cost per machine hour).

An unsuitable measure of performance for a profit centre is one that relates profits to capital employed (ROCE). ROCE could be a suitable performance measure for an investment centre.

23   D

Cost centre, profit centres and investment centres are often organised in a hierarchy, with several cost centres in a profit centre, several profit centres in an investment centre and several investment centres in an organisation. There will not be several profit centres (manager responsible for revenues and costs) in a cost centre (manager responsible for costs only).

24   C

If the budget period is one year, it would be inconvenient to wait up to one year to calculate the actual overhead costs of production retrospectively. Using a predetermined overhead rate gets round this problem, although as a consequence, there will be some under-absorbed or over-absorbed overheads.

25   C

This is a stepped cost. A stepped cost is a cost that is fixed within a certain range of activity levels, but then changes if the activity level rises above or falls below that range to a new 'fixed' level. In this example, supervision costs will rise as activity increases as more supervisory staff have to be employed.

26   B

	$	$
Sales revenue		320,000
Direct labour	100,000	
Direct material	75,000	
Production overhead	78,000	
	253,000	
		67,000
Other overhead costs		50,000
Profit		17,000

27   B

28   C

When forecasting it is key to understand cost behaviour

ANSWERS TO MOCK EXAM QUESTIONS : SECTION 4

29 A

Hannah's salary does not depend on whether or not she works on client work or doing general admin, hence her salary cost is fixed.

The fact that Hannah completes a timesheet allows her firm to apportion her salary costs to clients, hence her salary costs are direct.

30 C

Raw materials are a variable cost so the graph will begin at the origin and increase at a gradient equal to the cost per unit. The cost per unit falls at a certain point so the gradient will become less and the graph will be flatter. Option D shows a situation where the cost per unit becomes greater above a certain volume.

31 A

	Hours
Total hours worked	42
Idle time	6
Hours actively worked	36
Basic rate per hour	$8
Direct labour cost	$288

The overtime premium for the four hours of overtime, and the cost of the six hours of idle time, will be treated as an indirect labour cost.

32 C

Sales volume (units)	9,000
Raw materials units per product	2
	Units of material
Materials usage budget	18,000
Add closing inventory required	2,800
Less opening inventory available	(3,500)
Materials purchases (units)	17,300
Cost per unit	$5
Materials purchase budget in $	$86,500

33 B

Presumably, each employee receives the same benefits from the service, therefore the most suitable basis for apportioning the cost should be the number of employees in each department. Department A should therefore be charged with $1,800 × (10/20) = $900.

MA1 : MANAGEMENT INFORMATION

34 A

	$
Paid to employees	67,000
Employees' National Insurance contributions	21,000
Income tax	36,300
Gross pay	124,300
Employer's National Insurance contributions	13,200
Employer's contribution to employees' pension fund	15,000
Total labour cost	152,500

Gross earnings are the total earnings of employees. The employer must pay in addition the employer's National Insurance contributions, and if there is a pension scheme for employees, the employer's contributions into the scheme are also an additional labour cost.

35 D

The fixed production overhead absorption rate is $120,000/20,000 hours = $6 per direct labour hour.

	$
Direct materials (6 kg × $2.50)	15
Direct labour (2 hours × $4)	8
Variable production overhead (25% of 2 hours × $4)	2
Fixed production overhead (2 hours × $6)	12
Full production cost per unit	37

36 D

Kitchen fitting consists of short jobs for customers, with each job being different. A shipbuilder will operate a contract costing system, and an oil refinery and a steel producer are likely to have process costing systems.

37 B

Closing work-in-progress is 780 × 0.6 = 468.

Total equivalent units for the period are 5,640 + 468 = 6,108.

38 B

1,400 × $14.32 = $20,048

There are no losses in the process so there are 20,000 − 18,600 = 1,400 units of work-in-process. These are valued at $8.20 + $6.12 = $14.32.

ANSWERS TO MOCK EXAM QUESTIONS : SECTION 4

39 B

Receipts and issues

Units	Price per unit $	Cost $
100	5.00	500.0
150	5.50	825.0
———	———	———
250	5.30	1,325.0
(100)	5.30	(530.0)
———	———	———
150		795.0
100	6.00	600.0
———	———	———
250	5.58	1,395.0
(75)	5.58	(418.5)
———	———	———
175	5.58	**976.5**
———	———	———

40 A

FIFO means that the value of closing stock reflects the most recent prices paid.

41 B

× is not used for multiplication, the * symbol is.

42 C

(iii) is an advantage.

43 B

All are said to be advantages of spreadsheet software with the exception of (i) security. A computer-based approach exposes the firm to threats from viruses, hackers and general system failure.

44 D

45 D

A database can be used to organise operational data that allows different users to access the same files for their data processing requirements. An integrated accounts package is insufficient for handling all the operational data of an organisation.

46 B

Pie charts will be least effective to show trends but both of the others will work, although you could argue that the line chart is best.

MA1 : MANAGEMENT INFORMATION

47   B

The spreadsheet won't recognise the text 'TBC' as a number and will remind the user to input a number rather than text.

48   D

It would not be possible to select the hidden row as it is hidden. A user must select the rows above and below the hidden row or rows.

49   D

The formula in A is no use as it includes subtotals (e.g. cell C4) in the summation, resulting in figures effectively being double counted. B and C are no use as they deduct costs that have been entered as negative numbers (so need to be added).

50   A

Formatting is concerned with appearance and seeks to make the spreadsheet look more interesting and make it reflect the underlying data better. Thus a number format may be better than plain text (hence (4) is wrong). Formatting is not concerned with ordering, so statement (2) is incorrect.

FOUNDATIONS IN ACCOUNTANCY

Management Information

Specimen Exam applicable from June 2014

Paper MA1

Time allowed: 2 hours

ALL 50 questions are compulsory and MUST be attempted.

Do NOT open this paper until instructed by the supervisor.

This question paper must not be removed from the examination hall.

The Association of Chartered Certified Accountants

ALL 50 questions are compulsory and MUST be attempted

Please use the space provided on the inside cover of the Candidate Answer Booklet to indicate your chosen answer to each multiple choice question.
Each question is worth 2 marks.

1 Which of the following may be a cost centre?

    A One of the hotels owned by a leisure company
    B The accountancy department in a business
    C The direct material cost of a product
    D The total depreciation expense of a business

2 All of a company's workers are paid the same hourly rate.

The following spreadsheet is to be used to calculate wages earned by different workers each week. A formula is entered in cell B4 and then a fill command is used to copy this formula into cells C4 to G4.

	A	B	C	D	E	F	G
1	Wage rate per hour ($)	12					
2	Worker	P	Q	R	S	T	U
3	Hours worked	40	28	38	39	40	27
4	Wages earned ($)						
5							
6							

Which of the following formulae should be entered into cell B4 prior to using the fill command to make sure that the correct formulae is used for cells C4 to G4?

    A =B1*B3
    B =$B$1*B3
    C =B1*$B$3
    D =$B$1*$B*$3

3 There was no work-in-progress in a manufacturing process at the start of a period. 18,000 units of a product commenced processing in the period during which completed output was 16,100 units. The work-in-progress was 75% complete for conversion costs which were $4·60 per equivalent unit. There were no losses or gains in the process

What amount was included in the closing work-in-progress for conversion costs?

    A $6,555
    B $8,740
    C $11,653
    D $18,515

4 Which of the following statements is true?

    A Information consists of raw facts that have not been processed
    B Data consists of information
    C Data consists of processed information
    D Information consists of data which has been processed in a predefined way

5 For which of the following tasks would a computer spreadsheet be most useful?

- A Expense coding structure
- B Product listing
- C Staff appraisal
- D Cost analysis

6 Receipts and issues of a raw material for a period were:

	units	$ per unit	cumulative total $
Day 1 balance	160	3·70	592
Day 3 receipt	230	3·60	1,420
Day 5 issue	110		
Day 8 issue	150		

Using the LIFO inventory pricing method, what is the total cost of the issue on Day 8?

- A $540
- B $543
- C $545
- D $555

7 Product X is manufactured by Y Co. Direct materials cost $6·10 and prime costs total $9·60 per unit of product. Production overheads are absorbed at a rate of $13·40 per machine hour. Two units of Product X are manufactured per machine hour.

Using absorption costing, what is the total production cost per unit of Product X?

- A $16·30
- B $22·40
- C $23·00
- D $29·10

8 Which of the following is a major advantage of the use of computer spreadsheets in management accounting?

- A Formulas are consistent in that they usually appear as numbers
- B They can be printed and hard copies filed
- C They can be used to record the cost coding structure
- D What-if analysis can be carried out easily and quickly

9 Product X requires 1·8 kg of a raw material per finished unit. The material has a weight loss of 10% in preparation for manufacture. Inventory of the material is currently 420 kg but needs to be increased to 500 kg. 2,000 units of Product X are to be manufactured.

How many kg of the raw material need to be purchased to satisfy the above requirements?

- A 3,880
- B 3,920
- C 4,040
- D 4,080

10 At the end of a period the percentage completion of the work-in-progress in a continuous manufacturing process was over estimated.

What effect would correction of the error have on the cost per equivalent unit and the total cost of output completed in the period?

	Unit cost	Cost of output
A	Decrease	Decrease
B	Decrease	Increase
C	Increase	Decrease
D	Increase	Increase

11 What is the purpose of prime entry records?

- A Assist the preparation of a trial balance
- B Prevent unnecessary detail in the ledgers
- C Provide a check on the double-entry bookkeeping
- D Provide a list of outstanding payments

12 The following scatter graph plots nine observed sets of data from a factory.

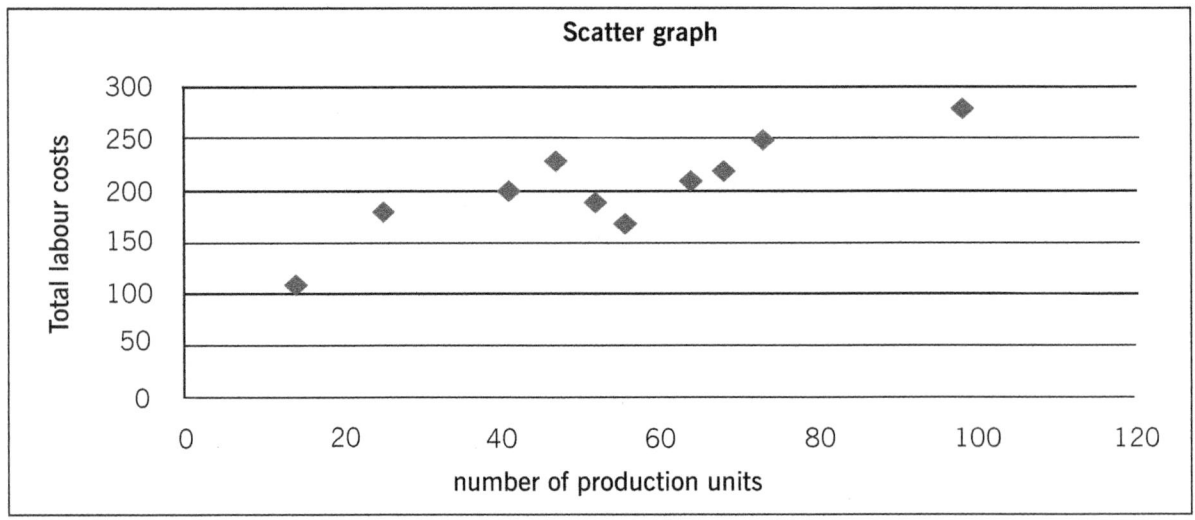

Which term would BEST describe the behaviour of total labour cost?

- A Fixed cost
- B Stepped – fixed cost
- C Semi-variable cost
- D Variable cost

13 A production operative is paid $11·00 per hour for a basic 35-hour week. Overtime is paid at 40% over the basic rate. The operative worked for 38 hours in week 9. Income tax deducted was $76·40 and benefit contribution payments were:

Employer $40
Employee   10% of gross pay

What was the net pay of the operative in week 9?

A $271·68
B $311·68
C $316·30
D $319·29

14 No losses or gains occur in a manufacturing process. There was no work-in-progress at the start of a period during which 9,600 litres of a raw material were input to the process. 8,700 litres of finished product were output from the process in the period. The stage of completion of the work-in-progress was:

Materials   100%
Conversion costs   60%

What were the equivalent units of production in the period?

	Materials	Conversion costs
A	8,700	8,700
B	8,700	9,060
C	9,600	9,240
D	9,600	9,600

15 Using marginal costing, what is the basis for valuing inventory of finished goods in a manufacturing business?

A   Direct + indirect production costs
B   Prime costs + total variable costs
C   Prime costs + variable production overheads
D   Production costs + variable non-production costs

16 What is a time sheet used for?

A   To calculate pay only
B   To charge cost centres for work done only
C   To record attendance time
D   To calculate pay and to charge cost centres for work done

17 Which of the following documents will MOST help a sales manager to monitor the effectiveness of a sales team?

A   A monthly report comparing sales targets with actual results
B   The sales department's organisational chart
C   A monthly report analysing the reasons for customer complaints
D   The completion of appraisal interview forms

18 The following financial figures relate to Jolly for a year:

	20X2 $
Sales	50,000
Cost of sales	(10,000)
Gross profit	40,000
Expenses	(15,000)
Net profit	25,000
Capital employed	100,000

What is the asset turnover ratio for 20X2?

A 0·8 times
B 0·4 times
C 2 times
D 0·5 times

19 The following spreadsheet shows a company's statement of profit or loss for the coming period.

	A	B	C	D	E
1	Statement of Profit or Loss				
2	Period 2				
3		Division A	Division B	DivisionC	Total
4	Sales Revenue	5,000	6,000	8,000	19,000
5	Variable costs	1,500	1,800	2,400	5,700
6	Contribution	3,500	4,200	5,600	13,300
7	Fixed cost	2,000	3,000	4,000	9,000
8	Profit	1,500	1,200	1,600	4,300
9					
10					

Which of the following formulae is correct for calculating the value of cell E8?

A =Sum(B8:D8)
B Sum(B8:D8)
C =Sum (E4:E7)
D Sum (E4:E7)

20 Which activity is LEAST likely to be the responsibility of the accounting function of a large organisation?

A Calculation of wages
B Control of trade receivables
C Dispatch of customer orders
D Payment of trade payables

21 A spreadsheet includes the following pie chart to analyse a company's total manufacturing cost for a period. The company's production overhead in the period was $124,700.

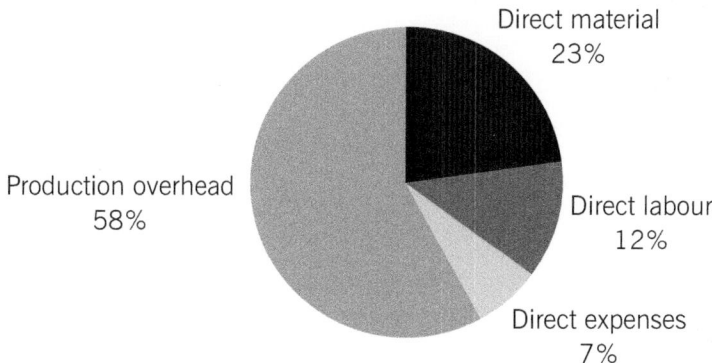

What are the total direct costs?

A $43,645
B $52,374
C $53,750
D $90,300

22 A Business has the following results:

	$
Sales	100,000
Cost of sales	(20,000)
Gross profit	80,000
Expenses	(30,000)
Net profit	50,000

What is the net profit margin for the Business?

A 50%
B 80%
C 62·5%
D 200%

23 What is the effect of using brackets in a spreadsheet formula?

A Divisions and multiplications are calculated before additions and subtractions
B Additions and subtractions are calculated before divisions and multiplications
C The contents of the brackets are calculated first
D The contents of the brackets are calculated last

24 B $156

25 A To demonstrate formal relationships and communication flows

26 C $26,241

27 A Management Accountant wishes to present the following spreadsheet information in a chart.

	Direct cost	Production overheads	Non-production overheads	Total cost
Factory 1	80	30	30	140
Factory 2	200	50	40	290
Factory 3	70	20	40	130

She is considering using the following charts:

(i) Scatter diagram
(ii) Line chart
(iii) Stacked (compound) bar chart

Which chart(s) would be most appropriate?

A (i) and (iii)
B (ii)
C (iii)
D (i) and (ii) only

28 The following indirect costs were incurred in a factory in a period:

Rental of premises $80,000
Utilities $25,000

There are two cost centres, A and B, in the factory which between them occupy the 20,000 square metres (sq m) of floor space (cost centre A, 8,000 sq m; cost centre B, 12,000 sq m).

What is the total indirect cost apportionment to cost centre B in the period if floor space is used as the basis of apportionment?

A $42,000
B $52,500
C $63,000
D $105,000

29 You have been asked to write a report outlining the qualities of good information.

Which of the following would you NOT include in the report?

A The information should be complete
B The information should be communicated via an appropriate channel
C The information should be understandable
D The information should be communicated to everyone in the organisation

30 In an interlocking accounting system what would be the entry for the issue of indirect material?

A Dr Raw material inventory   Cr Work in progress
B Dr Raw material inventory   Cr Production overhead
C Dr Work in progress   Cr Raw material inventory
D Dr Production overhead   Cr Raw material inventory

31 A coding system uses a combination of letters and numbers to classify costs. The first two digits of each code represent the cost centre, the third and fourth digits represent the type of expense and the fifth and sixth digits represent the detail of the expense.

Relevant codes for a particular expense are:

	code
Selling expense	24
Northern division	ND
Commission	SC

What is the correct code for the above expense?

- **A** SC24ND
- **B** NDSC24
- **C** ND24SC
- **D** 24SCND

32 Which of the following are reasons for formatting data in a spreadsheet?

(1) To get data into the correct order for analysis
(2) To make labels visually interesting
(3) To make numbers more descriptive of what they represent
(4) To make the data appear as plain text

- **A** 1 and 3 only
- **B** 2 and 3 only
- **C** 2 and 4 only
- **D** 1, 2 and 3

33 Direct operatives in a factory are paid on a time rate basis for a 35-hour week.

If productivity can be improved what will happen to direct labour costs per unit of output?

- **A** Decrease
- **B** Increase
- **C** No change
- **D** Not possible to determine from the information provided

34 Which of the following statements concerning spreadsheet cells are correct?

(1) A formula in a particular cell may calculate numbers for several cells
(2) Clicking on a particular cell, and then entering a number or text, will enter data into that single cell
(3) Each cell can contain a number, a label or a formula
(4) Press Shift and Enter to select the cell below in the same column

- **A** 1, 2 and 4
- **B** 1, 3 and 4
- **C** 2 and 3 only
- **D** 3 and 4 only

35 Which of the following statements concerning the recording and analysis of sales are TRUE?

(1) The sales figure that should be taken from an invoice is net of both trade discount and sales tax
(2) Sales may be analysed in a number of different ways for management accounting purposes

A Both 1 and 2
B 1 only
C 2 only
D Neither 1 nor 2

36 Which of the following are features of useful management information?

(1) Communicated to the right person
(2) Provided whatever the cost
(3) Sufficiently accurate for its cost

A (1) only
B (1) and (3) only
C (2) and (3) only
D (1), (2) and (3)

37 Which item would most likely be treated as an indirect cost by a furniture manufacturer?

A Fabric to cover the seat of a chair
B Metal used for the legs of a chair
C Staples to fit the fabric to the seat of a chair
D Wood used to make the frame of a chair

38 Which of the following is TRUE about the effect of different methods of pricing raw materials from inventory in a period of consistently rising prices?

(1) Production costs will be higher using FIFO rather than LIFO
(2) Closing inventory values will be lower using periodic weighted average rather than cumulative weighted average

A 1 only
B 2 only
C Both statements
D Neither statement

39 In an inventory control system, what is normally meant by free inventory?

A Inventory which is available for new orders from customers
B Inventory which is available for promotional offers
C Inventory which is in transit from supplier to warehouse
D Inventory which is in transit from warehouse to customer

40 What is the charging of an overhead cost directly to a cost centre known as?

A Overhead absorption
B Overhead allocation
C Overhead apportionment
D Overhead assignment

41 Which of the following states the responsibility of the manager of a profit centre?

- **A** Responsibility for revenues but not costs
- **B** Responsibility for costs but not revenues
- **C** Responsibility for revenues and costs
- **D** Responsibility for revenues, costs and investment

42 Which of the following defines cost classification?

- **A** The grouping of costs according to their common characteristics
- **B** The allotment of items of cost to cost centres
- **C** The sum of all costs incurred
- **D** The use by several companies of the same costing methods

43 Which of the following are correct descriptions applied to computer spreadsheets?

(1) An entire page of rows and columns is called a workbook
(2) Each row is identified by a letter
(3) Data is organised in rows and columns
(4) The intersection of each row and column defines a cell

- **A** 1 and 2 only
- **B** 2 and 4 only
- **C** 3 and 4 only
- **D** 1, 2, 3 and 4

44 Production labour costs incurred during a period included the following items:

(1) Salary of factory manager $2,400
(2) Training of direct workers $1,660
(3) Normal idle time $840
(4) Overtime premiums of direct workers $2,760
(5) Overtime hours of direct workers at basic rate $9,200

What total amount would usually be charged to production overhead for the above items?

- **A** $4,060
- **B** $4,900
- **C** $7,660
- **D** $16,860

45 Which of the following are features of an efficient and effective coding system?

(1) Each item should have a unique code
(2) Each code should contain a combination of letters and numbers
(3) Each code should completely disguise the item being coded
(4) Codes should not be uniform in length and structure

- **A** 1 only
- **B** 1 and 2 only
- **C** 1, 3 and 4 only
- **D** 2, 3 and 4 only

46 Which of the following is normally treated as a direct labour cost?

  A Controllable idle time
  B Uncontrollable idle time
  C Overtime premium due to a temporary backlog in production
  D Overtime premium at the specific request of a customer

47 25,000 units of a company's single product are produced in a period during which 28,000 units are sold. Opening inventory was 7,000 units. Unit costs of the product are:

	$ per unit
Direct costs	16·20
Fixed production overhead	7·60
Fixed non-production overhead	2·90

  What is the difference in profit between absorption and marginal costing?

  A $22,800
  B $30,400
  C $31,500
  D $42,000

48 A sales representative earns a basic salary of $10,000 per annum, a guaranteed end-of-year bonus of $5,000 and 5% commission on the value of sales.

  What cost classification is appropriate for the sales representative's salary?

  A Direct cost
  B Product cost
  C Semi-fixed cost
  D Prime cost

49 Consider the following tasks:

  (1) Setting selling prices for products and services
  (2) Analysing departmental expenditure for control purposes
  (3) Calculating the quantity of raw materials in store
  (4) Calculating wages for employees working on special shifts

  Which tasks are likely to be carried out by a trainee accountant?

  A 1 and 2 only
  B 1, 3 and 4 only
  C 2, 3 and 4 only
  D 1, 2, 3 and 4

50 TRS CONSULTANTS
31 Oxford Avenue
Milton Mewbury
Lincolnshire

Invoice number: 9911

Date: 25 February 20X1

Customer:
Jacqueline Smith
ACCA
2 Central Quay
Glasgow
G3 8BW

Item:
Accountancy training $1,500·00

In the integrated computerised accounts of TRS Consultants, which of the following is correct?

- **A** The bank account will be credited
- **B** The sales account will be debited
- **C** Trade payables control account will be debited
- **D** Trade receivables control account will be debited

(100 marks)

End of Question Paper

Answers

FOUNDATIONS IN ACCOUNTANCY – Paper MA1
Management Information

Specimen Exam Answers

1 B
2 B
3 A
   (18,000 – 16,100)*·75*$4·60 = 6,555
4 D
5 D
6 B
   ((230 – 110)*3·60) + (3·7*(150 – (230 – 110))) = $543
7 A
   Overhead costs per unit:
   13·4 ÷ 2 = 6·7
   Total production cost per unit:
   6·7 + 9·60 = 16·30
8 D
9 D
   Material required per finished unit with a 10% loss:
   1·8 ÷ ·90 = 2
   Total material required for manufacture:
   2*2,000 = 4,000
   Total materials to buy:
   4,000 – 420 + 500 = 4,080
10 D
11 B
12 C
13 B
   Basic pay (35*11) = 385
   Overtime pay (11*1·40)*(38 – 35) = 46·2
   Gross pay (385 + 46·20) = 431·20
   Benefit contribution (431·2*·1) = 43·12
   Net pay ($431·20 – $76·40 – $43·12) = $311·68
14 C
   Output 8,700
   WIP (9,600 – 8,700) = 900
   Equivalent units:

	Material costs	Conversion costs
Finished goods	8,700	8700
WIP	900 (900*100%)	540 (900* 60%)
Total	9,600	9,240

15 C
16 D
17 A
18 D
   Sales/capital employed
   50,000/100,000
   0·5 times
19 A
20 C
21 D
   Total direct costs percentage: (23 + 12 + 7) = 42%
   Total direct costs: (124,700/58%) *42% = $90,300
22 A
   (Net profit/ sales)*100
   (50,000/100,000)*100
   50%
23 C

24 B
Day 1 pay (100*0·5) = $50
Day 2 pay (90*0·5) = 40 but get minimum = $50
+ day 3 pay (100*0·5) + (10*0·6) = $56
Total = $156

25 A

26 C
Overhead production cost for Job 1
(4,360/(4,360 + 2,940))*9,855 = $5,886
Total costs (5,269 + 10,726 + 4,360 + 5,886) = $26,241

27 C

28 C
Percentage occupancy for centre B
12,000/(8,000 + 12,000) = 60%
Overheads apportioned to B
(80,000 + 25,000)*60%
$63,000

29 D

30 D

31 C

32 B

33 A

34 C

35 A

36 B

37 C

38 B

39 A

40 B

41 C

42 A

43 C

44 C
(2,400 + 1,660 + 840 + 2,760) = 7,660

45 A

46 D

47 A

48 C

49 C

50 D